LET'S BAKE!

CATHRYN DRESSER

Orion
Children's Books

CONTENTS

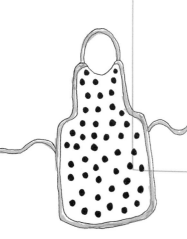

Hi everyone!

I'm Cathryn Dresser and my favourite things in the world are: my *family*, BAKING, the Great British Bake Off, and **CHOCOLATE!**

Let me tell you what else is I think is brilliant - the four seasons. The sunshine, showers and flowers in spring, the warm, light evenings in SUMMER, bonfire night in the **autumn** (oh, and my birthday!), and the most wonderful time of the year... Christmas, in WINTER.

In this book you will find a collection of easy and delicious recipes inspired by the time of year, whether it's because of an occasion or an ingredient. But you can make any of the recipes whenever you fancy, because this is your book!

I hope you have as much fun baking with your family and friends as I have had putting these recipes together especially for YOU. I know that before long you will all get the baking bug and be Star Bakers in no time!

So have fun, make, create, laugh, share, eat and...

Let's Bake!

Cathryn x

THE TRICKY BITS

DUSTING THE WORKTOP WITH FLOUR

Take a small handful of flour and sprinkle lightly across your worktop before you start rolling dough. This will help stop your dough sticking.

RUBBING BUTTER INTO FLOUR

Add cold, diced butter to the flour.

Using your fingertips and thumbs, take small amounts of the mixture and start rubbing them together.

Keep rubbing until the mixture looks like breadcrumbs.

CRACKING AND SEPARATING EGGS

Set out two bowls.

Crack your egg gently on the rim of a bowl, then use your thumbs to prise the two halves of the egg apart.

Put your hand over one of the bowls, palm facing up, and let the whites drip through the spaces between your fingers until all that is left is the yolk in your hand.

MELTING CHOCOLATE IN DOUBLE BOILER

Break the chocolate into small pieces and place in a heatproof bowl.

Add boiling water to a saucepan and put on a medium heat so it is just simmering.

Place your bowl over the top of the saucepan, making sure the base of the bowl does not touch the water.

Heat the chocolate, stirring gently once or twice, until melted.

MAKING A WELL IN DRY INGREDIENTS

When all of your dry ingredients are together in your bowl, dig a hole in the middle of them to make a well. This is where you pour your wet ingredients.

FOLDING

Use a metal spoon to carefully cut through your mixture, stirring and turning your spoon in a figure of eight motion.

TESTING WHETHER A CAKE IS COOKED

 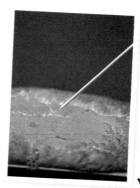

Carefully stick a skewer into the middle of your cake. If it comes out clean, your cake is ready. If not, pop it back into the oven for another 5 minutes, then check again.

✗   ✓

CREAMING TOGETHER BUTTER AND SUGAR

Make sure the butter is at room temperature before you start. Using a wooden spoon or electric mixer, start mixing slowly and get faster as the mixture becomes softer and smoother.

It's ready when it turns pale and looks like this.

KNEADING DOUGH

NOT QUITE READY YET!

  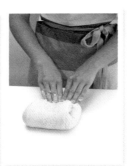  

Place the dough on a lightly floured surface and flatten it out.

Then fold the dough in half towards you and flatten again.

Give the dough a quarter turn. Repeat.

Continue for about 10 minutes until smooth, springy and elastic.

RECIPE FOR BAKING SUCCESS

INGREDIENTS

A generous handful of **fun**

A spoonful of **concentration**

A pinch of **creativity**

A sprinkle of **patience**

A dash of **love**

HOW TO DO IT

1. Mix all the ingredients in a big bowl of confidence, with a fearless spoon, pour into a tin of happiness and bake in a hot, hopeful oven until practically perfect in every way.

2. Share with everyone and enjoy!

THINGS TO REMEMBER

1. **Wash your hands.** This is super important to stop the spreading of germs.

2. **Be prepared.** Make sure you have all your ingredients laid out and ready to go when you need them.

3. **Preheat your oven** at the right time and to the right temperature. This will help you get your bakes spot-on.

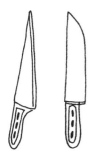

4. **Tidy as you go.** This will keep you organised and focused and give you great baking results.

5. **Always have an adult on hand** to do the jobs that are not safe for you to do on your own. Ovens are hot and knifes can be sharp.

6. **Enjoy it** and don't worry if things go wrong – we all have baking hiccups, and practice really does make perfect.

SPRING

CHARMING CHEESE AND CHIVE BISCUITS

PREP TIME: 30 minutes **BAKE TIME:** 10–12 minutes

These little cheese biscuits are magically quick and simple to make. They are perfect for parties, picnics, snacks and lunchboxes, and are sure to put a smile on people's faces – charming, in fact!

MAKES ABOUT 20 BISCUITS

100g **Cheddar cheese**, grated

50g **plain flour** or white spelt flour, plus extra for dusting

25g **wholemeal flour**

25g **unsalted butter**

50g **Parmesan cheese**, grated, plus extra for sprinkling

2 tablespoons fresh **chives**, chopped or snipped

YOU WILL NEED

☐ Food processor
☐ Weighing scales
☐ Cling film
☐ Rolling pin
☐ Cookie cutters (we like these best as little mice, circles or stars)
☐ Baking tray
☐ Non-stick baking parchment
☐ Cooling rack

1. Preheat the oven to 190°C/170°C fan/gas mark 5. Line one or two baking trays with non-stick baking parchment.

2. Put the Cheddar, both flours, butter and the Parmesan in a food processor and blitz until it begins to stick together and form a ball of dough. This may take a few minutes – so be patient. Add the chives and blitz a bit more.

3. Ask an adult to remove the blade from the food processor, scrape out your dough and roll it into a ball. Then flatten it into a disc, wrap it in cling film and put in the fridge for 15 minutes.

4. Take the dough out of the fridge. Lightly dust your worktop with flour, then roll out the dough until it is about as thick as a pound coin. Use your cookie cutters to cut out your biscuits. Place the shapes carefully on your lined baking tray.

5. Ask an adult to help you put the baking tray in the oven. Bake for 10–12 minutes, or until golden. When an adult removes the cookies from the oven, put them on a wire rack to cool.

STORAGE: These can be stored in an airtight container for up to a week.

Working by hand?

If you don't have a food processor, all you need to do is put the flours, cheeses and butter in a bowl and use your fingers to pinch and rub the mixture together. Use a wooden spoon to stir through the chives. Now, add a little (about one third) of a beaten free-range egg and stir it together to form a dough. Wrap and chill as with the other method and continue in the same way.

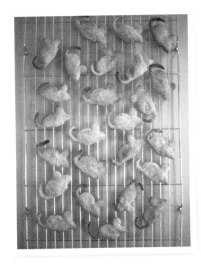

☆ Top Tip! ☆

When rolling out the dough,
divide it into 4 pieces and do one
at a time. This makes it easier
to roll and keeps the other
dough from getting too warm.

LIGHTHOUSE KEEPER'S SALMON AND SPINACH PARCELS

PREP TIME: 15 minutes (or 45 minutes if making your own pastry)

BAKE TIME: 30 minutes

One of my favourite children's books is called *The Lighthouse Keeper's Lunch*. Mrs Grinling, the lighthouse keeper's wife, makes the loveliest lunches in the world and sends them on a rope from their cottage all the way over the sea to the lighthouse. These parcels are exactly the sort of thing I can imagine she'd make.

MAKES 4 PARCELS

Unsalted butter, for greasing

100g **cream cheese**

65g **baby spinach**

Zest of ½ a **lemon** (optional)

Pinch of **salt** and **pepper**

Pinch of **grated nutmeg** (optional)

4 **salmon fillets**, skinless and boneless

1 tablespoon **plain flour**, for dusting

1 x 500g pack of shop-bought **shortcrust pastry** (or make your own, see recipe over page)

1 free-range **egg**, beaten

YOU WILL NEED

☐ Baking tray
☐ Food processor
☐ Kitchen paper
☐ Weighing scales
☐ Pastry brush
☐ Fork

1. Preheat the oven to 190°C/170°C fan/gas mark 5. Lightly grease a baking tray.

2. Put the cream cheese and spinach in a food processor, then blitz until you have a creamy green paste. Add the lemon zest, salt and pepper, and nutmeg, if using, then set aside. Pat the salmon fillets dry with a piece of kitchen paper.

3. Lightly dust the worktop with flour, then divide your pastry into 4 equal pieces. Roll out each piece to form a rectangle that is about 6-8cm longer and a little more than twice as wide as your salmon fillet.

4. Take your first pastry rectangle and imagine it is like an open book. Lay one of the salmon fillets on the right 'page' side, but don't put the fish too close to the edge of the pastry.

5. Spread one quarter of the spinach mixture on top of the salmon and brush all around the edges of the pastry with beaten egg. Fold the left 'page' side of the pastry over the salmon, as if closing the book.

6. Use the side of your hand to gently seal the pastry, then go around the edges pushing down with the prongs of a fork to seal completely – this stops the filling leaking out and also makes it look pretty.

7. Brush the top of your pastry parcel with more of the beaten egg, then prick the top with a fork in 3 or 4 places. Repeat with the remaining pieces of salmon and pastry, then move all 4 sealed pastry parcels to the prepared baking tray.

8. Bake in the preheated oven for 25–30 minutes until golden brown.

STORAGE: Eat immediately with new potatoes and peas. Yum!

SOURED CREAM PASTRY

If you want to make your own pastry, follow this easy recipe.

MAKES ENOUGH FOR 4 PARCELS
300g **plain flour**
Pinch of **salt**
150g cold **unsalted butter**, cut into small cubes
60ml **soured cream**

YOU WILL NEED
☐ Mixing bowls
☐ Wooden spoon
☐ Cling film

1. Tip the flour into a bowl and add the salt and butter. Use your fingertips to squash and rub in the butter until the mixture looks like breadcrumbs.

2. Stir in the soured cream a little at a time, until you have a soft ball of dough. If it feels too dry, add a bit more soured cream. If it's too sticky, add a sprinkle more of flour. Wrap the pastry in cling film and chill in the fridge for 30 minutes.

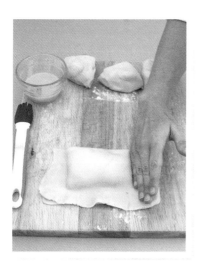

DIPPY BAKED EGGS WITH SOLDIERS

PREP TIME: 5 minutes **BAKE TIME:** 12 minutes

These make a delicious morning or teatime treat. They are even easier than boiling an egg, and are a great breakfast in bed for Mother's Day. They go perfectly with the hot buttered soldiers.

SERVES 1

A large knob of **unsalted butter**, to butter the ramekin and to spread on your soldiers

1 large free-range **egg**

1 tablespoon **single cream** or full fat milk

Pinch of **salt** (optional)

Pinch of **white pepper** (optional)

A slice of **bread**

YOU WILL NEED

☐ A ramekin dish (a small dish about the size of a small tin of baked beans)

☐ Baking tray

☐ Toaster or grill

☐ Knife

HOW TO DO IT

1. Preheat the oven to 180°C/160°C fan/gas mark 4. Butter the inside of the ramekin.

2. Crack the egg into the ramekin and spoon the cream or milk over the top. Add a pinch of salt and pepper to season, if you like.

3. Put the ramekin on a baking tray and ask an adult to help you put it into the oven. Bake for about 12 minutes. After 10 minutes ask an adult to gently press the top of the egg to check if it is cooked and that the yolk is still dippy.

4. Prepare your soldiers by toasting your bread, then spreading with butter and cutting into strips.

STORAGE: Eat straight away, remembering to be careful of the hot ramekin.

☆ Top Tip! ☆
Try adding some chopped ham, cooked mushrooms, cooked chopped tomatoes or grated cheese.

WELSH RAREBIT PINWHEELS

PREP TIME: 15 minutes   **BAKE TIME:** 15-20 minutes

Little cheese-on-toast-inspired pinwheels that are fun to make and best served warm.

MAKES 10

A little **oil**, to grease the baking tray

25g **unsalted butter**

25g **plain flour**, plus a little extra for dusting

100ml **milk**

200g **Cheddar cheese**, grated

2 teaspoons **wholegrain mustard** (optional)

1 tablespoon **Worcestershire sauce**

Pinch of **black pepper**

1 x 375g pack of shop-bought ready-rolled **puff pastry**

1 medium free-range **egg**, beaten

YOU WILL NEED

☐ 2 baking trays
☐ Grater
☐ Small saucepan
☐ Wooden spoon
☐ Balloon whisk
☐ Mixing bowl
☐ Cling film
☐ Pastry brush
☐ Knife

HOW TO DO IT

1. Preheat the oven to 200°C/180°C fan/gas mark 6. Grease the baking trays.

2. With the help of an adult, melt the butter in a small saucepan over a low heat. Now stir in the flour with a wooden spoon. Keep stirring for about 2 minutes, then swap your spoon for a whisk and begin to add the milk to the pan slowly. Keep whisking as the sauce thickens.

3. When your sauce is thick and smooth, remove it from the heat, add the cheese, mustard (if using), Worcestershire sauce and pepper, and stir. Spoon the mixture into a bowl, cover with cling film and leave to cool for a few minutes.

4. Dust the worktop with a little flour and lay out your pastry sheet. Spread the mixture over the pastry leaving a 2cm border all the way around. Brush the border with the beaten egg, then roll up the pastry sheet, starting from the short side. Trim both ends so it is neat (you can bake these trimmings too so don't throw them away). Wrap the rolled up pastry in cling film and put in the fridge to chill for 20–30 minutes.

5. Take your roll out of the fridge and ask an adult to help you cut it into 10 slices. Lay the pinwheels flat on your baking tray and brush them with the remaining egg.

6. Ask an adult to put the baking tray in the oven and bake for 15–20 minutes, until golden.

STORAGE: They are best eaten on the day they have been made, as the filling can make the pastry go a little soggy. However, you can store them in the fridge for 3 days and re-heat them for 10 or so minutes in a hot oven.

⊚ Try Something Different! ⊚
You can use this pinwheel idea with all sorts of different fillings. Why not try mozzarella, ham and mushrooms? Or even marzipan and cherry jam?

Cathryn Says:
Eat these pinwheels as part of a springtime lunch with salad, or hot from the oven with baked beans for tea.

CHEESE AND MARMITE HELTER- SKELTERS

PREP TIME: 15 minutes **BAKE TIME:** 20 minutes

These are the ultimate cheese twists. In my house, we can't resist the combination of Marmite and cheese, especially on toast, so that's where this recipe comes from. They're called helter-skelters because that's what they look like when they are twisted and baked.

MAKES 12

2 tablespoons **Marmite**

15g **unsalted butter**

1 tablespoon **plain flour**, for dusting

1 x 375g pack of shop-bought ready-rolled **puff pastry**

150g **Cheddar cheese**, grated

YOU WILL NEED

☐ 2 baking trays
☐ Non-stick baking parchment
☐ Pastry brush
☐ Rolling pin
☐ Sharp knife

HOW TO DO IT

1. Preheat the oven to 200°C/180°C fan/gas mark 6. Line the baking trays with non-stick baking parchment.

2. With the help of an adult, melt the Marmite and butter in a small saucepan over a low heat until runny. Leave to cool for a minute or two. Meanwhile, lightly dust the worktop with flour and lay out the pastry sheet, with the short side facing towards you.

3. Using a pastry brush, spread the Marmite mixture over the pastry, then sprinkle the cheese over the top two thirds, leaving a space at the end closest to you.

4. Fold the non-cheesy bit of the pastry up so it covers half of the cheesy section. Then fold again in the same way. You should now have a neatly-folded rectangle of pastry.

5. Sprinkle a bit more flour on the worktop, then roll out the pastry again into a rectangle that is a similar size to the one you started with.

6. Place your pastry with the longest side closest to you, and cut into 6 equal strips. Cut each of these rectangles in half from one corner to the opposite corner so you end up with 12 long, pointed triangles. Take each of your long triangle pieces and twist them from the top pointy corner.

7. Put your twisted pastry pieces on the prepared baking tray and ask an adult to put it in the oven. Bake for 20 minutes, until golden.

   STORAGE: These are nicest eaten on the day they are made, but you can store them in an airtight container for up to 3 days.

Cathryn Says:

P.S. If you don't like Marmite, you can just leave it out - but promise you'll try them with it once first!

☆ Top Tip! ☆

Twist the pastry into the
helter-skelter shape on
the baking tray so that
you don't have to move
the shapes before putting
them in the oven.

Spring 33

WONDERFUL WHITE LOAF

PREP TIME: 30 minutes   **BAKE TIME:** 30 minutes

The smell of baking bread is the best in the world. Everybody thinks that baking bread is tricky - it isn't! It just takes a bit of time. So when the April showers arrive (and they will), and you're stuck inside with nothing to do, get bread baking. I promise you, the time it takes is well worth it.

MAKES 1 LOAF

500g **strong white flour**, plus a little extra for dusting

1 x 7g sachet of **fast-action yeast**

Large pinch of **salt**

300ml **warm water**

2 tablespoons **olive oil**, plus a little extra for greasing

YOU WILL NEED

☐ Weighing scales
☐ 1 or 2 large mixing bowls
☐ Cling film
☐ 1 x 900g loaf tin
☐ Measuring jug
☐ Baking tray
☐ Cooling rack

P.S. Try a slice with butter and homemade strawberry jam (p217)

1. You preheat the oven later in this recipe. Look out for it in Step 7. You also need a large, lightly-oiled bowl and cling film ready for when your loaf needs to prove (or rise) and a warm place to keep it. Grease your loaf tin with a little oil and dust lightly with flour.

2. Put the flour into your other bowl, then add the yeast on one side and the salt on the other. Make a well in the centre of the dry ingredients and pour in the water and oil.

3. Using one hand, mix the flour into the water and oil – just imagine your hand is a big spoon! Keep mixing until all the ingredients have come together and you have a sticky dough.

4. Lightly dust the worktop with flour, tip out the dough, then roll up your sleeves and knead for at least 15 minutes. You might need someone else to take turns, as it's hard work and your arms will be ready to drop off! After 15 minutes, you should have a smooth, stretchy, soft ball of dough.

5. Put the dough into your lightly-oiled bowl and cover with cling film. Put this somewhere warm (but not hot) and leave to rise for 1–2 hours, until it doubles in size.

6. Lightly dust the worktop again, take the dough out of the bowl and knead for 1 minute. Shape it into an oval and carefully place in your prepared loaf tin. Put the tin on a baking tray, cover with some greased cling film and put it back in its warm spot for a further 30 minutes.

7. Preheat the oven to its maximum temperature (usually 230°C/210°C fan/gas mark 8). Take your loaf from its warm spot and dust with a little flour, then ask an adult to put into the oven. When your loaf has been in the oven for 10 minutes, turn the oven down to 200°C/180°C/gas mark 6 and bake for a further 15–20 minutes, until golden.

8. Ask an adult to remove from the oven and turn your loaf out of its tin onto a wire rack to cool.

STORAGE: Freshly home-baked bread is best eaten within 2 or a maximum of 3 days. If you do have some left over, don't throw it away – use it for the Banana Sandwich Custard Pud' on page 186.

@ Try Something Different! @

This basic recipe can be used to make all kinds of breads, and rolls too. To make rolls simple divide and shape into 6 rounds and bake for slightly less time.

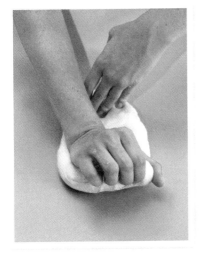

SUPER SCONES

PREP TIME: 10 minutes   **BAKE TIME:** 12 minutes

My mum always says, 'Scones: 7 minutes to make, 7 minutes to bake.' This is not completely true, but it isn't far off. They are a super-easy teatime treat. I have included a basic recipe and two variations here: one sweet and one savoury – both super!

MAKES ABOUT 16 SCONES

450g **self-raising flour**, plus a little extra for dusting

2 teaspoons **baking powder**

Pinch of **salt**

100g **unsalted butter**, cut into small cubes

75g **caster sugar** (only if making a sweet version)

260ml **full-fat milk**

1 medium free-range **egg**, beaten

YOU WILL NEED
☐ Weighing scales
☐ Baking tray
☐ Sieve
☐ Large mixing bowl
☐ Measuring jug
☐ Fork
☐ Metal knife
☐ Pastry or cookie cutter
☐ Pastry brush
☐ Cooling rack

HOW TO DO IT

1. Preheat the oven to 220°C/200°C fan/gas mark 7. Lightly flour a baking tray.

2. Sift the flour and baking powder into your bowl, then add the salt and stir. Add the butter and use your fingertips to break up and rub in the butter until the mixture looks like breadcrumbs. If you're making sweet scones, add the sugar now too.

3. In a measuring jug, combine the milk and egg and beat with a fork. Now, in your bowl, make a well in the middle of the flour and pour three-quarters of the egg and milk mixture into the well.

4. Use a metal butter or palette knife to cut through the mixture. You want to cut through the liquid and drag the flour down into it, stirring a little as you go. Continue until the mixture starts to form a dough. Add a tiny bit more milk if it feels dry. Then use your hands to bring the dough together completely.

5. Lightly dust the worktop with flour and tip out your dough. Gently flatten it with the palms of your hands until it is a nice round disc about 3–4cm thick.

6. Now it's time to cut out your scones. Dip your cutter into the flour to stop it sticking, then cut as many shapes as you can and put them on the dusted baking tray.

7. Gather the remaining dough and gently press together to cut more scones. Repeat until all the dough has been used up.

8. Brush the tops of your scones with the leftover egg and milk mixture. Ask an adult to put the tray in the preheated oven and bake the scones for 10–12 minutes, until golden and well-risen.

STORAGE: Scones are best enjoyed fresh and eaten within 2 days.

@ For Hot-Cross Scones @

Add 2 teaspoons of mixed spice with the flour. Then, when you stir in the sugar, add the grated zest of half an orange and 125g sultanas and follow the same basic recipe. Before you put them in the oven, mix 50g flour with 3 tablespoons of water, and use this to decorate the top of your scones with a cross. These are best warm, with lots of butter and honey!

@ For Cheesy Ploughman's Scones @

Just replace the sugar with 100g grated Cheddar cheese and the milk with 2 tablespoons of small chunk pickle. Then follow the same basic recipe. These are great with cheese, ham and salad for a lovely lunch.

BRILLIANT BAPS AND ICED BUNS FOR TEA

PREP TIME: 30 minutes plus 1½ hours proving/rising

BAKE TIME: 15 minutes

This marvellous recipe is two in one. The first is for Brilliant Baps, which can be used for lunches, picnics and burger buns. Then, by simply adding more sugar to the dough and covering the tops with icing, you have the most scrumptious Iced Buns for tea.

MAKES 12 LARGE BAPS OR BUNS

600g **strong white flour**, plus a little extra for dusting

1 teaspoon **salt**

50g **unsalted butter**, cold and cut into 1cm cubes

1½ x 7g sachets of **fast-action yeast** (about 11–12g total)

1 tablespoon **caster sugar**

1 large free-range **egg**

300ml **milk**, warmed gently in a pan or the microwave

FOR ICED BUNS:

50g **caster sugar**

350g **icing sugar**

6 tablespoons **water**

YOU WILL NEED

☐ Weighing scales
☐ Baking tray
☐ Large mixing bowl
☐ Measuring jug
☐ Fork
☐ Wooden spoon
☐ Kitchen paper

HOW TO DO IT

1. Lightly dust a baking tray with flour. Look out for the preheat the oven stage at Step 9.

2. Heat the milk and butter in a pan, over a low heat until the milk is warm and the butter has melted.

3. Put the flour, salt, sugar and yeast in a large mixing bowl and stir together. Then make a well in the middle.

4. In a jug, beat your egg with a fork, then add to the warmed milk and butter. Pour into the well in your flour mix and stir with a wooden spoon. You want to cut through the liquid and drag the flour down into it, stirring a little as you go. Do this until the mixture starts to come together and you have a sticky dough.

5. Lightly dust the worktop with flour, tip the dough out and knead for 10 minutes, until smooth, soft and stretchy.

6. Wipe out the bowl in which you made the dough and put your dough back in. Cover with cling film and leave in a warm place for 1 hour, until it has doubled in size.

7. Now take the dough out of the bowl and divide into 12 equal pieces. Shape each piece of dough into a ball. Place your balls of dough in neat rows close together on the prepared baking tray.

8. Cover with a greased bit of cling film and put back into your warm spot for another 30 minutes, until they have doubled in size again. Now they are ready to bake!

9. While you're waiting for your dough to rise, preheat the oven to 200°C/180°C fan/gas mark 6. Ask an adult to put the tray in the oven and bake for 10–15 minutes, until they are golden and sound slightly hollow when tapped underneath (ask an adult to do this).

10. Ask an adult to remove from the oven and set aside on a wire rack to cool. Tear apart and enjoy.

STORAGE: Store in an airtight container and eat within 2–3 days.

IF YOU'RE MAKING ICED BUNS

1. Follow the same recipe but add an extra 50g caster sugar to the flour and yeast. Then, at the end of Step 7, roll each dough ball into a fat finger bun and continue from Step 9.

2. For the icing, put the icing sugar into a bowl and add the water, a little at a time. Stir until you have a thick, smooth paste.

3. When your buns have cooled, dip them one at a time into the icing, then smooth it on with a spoon.

PERFECT FOR ANY CELEBRATION VANILLA SPONGE

PREP TIME: 15 minutes   **BAKE TIME:** 35 minutes

This recipe is one you will use ALL the time. It is the loveliest cake and perfect for all sorts of celebrations. It's delicious just filled with jam and buttercream, or let your creative side go wild and decorate as imaginatively as you dare!

MAKES 1 LARGE 23CM SANDWICH SPONGE

FOR THE CAKE:

300g **margarine**, plus a little extra for greasing

300g **caster sugar**

1 ½ teaspoon **vanilla paste** or extract

6 free-range **eggs** (at room temperature)

300g **self-raising flour**

1 teaspoon **baking powder**

Icing sugar, for dusting

FOR THE BUTTERCREAM:

200g **unsalted butter**, very soft

400g **icing sugar**, plus extra for dusting

½ teaspoon **vanilla extract**

1 tablespoon **milk**

½ jar of **good-quality jam** (I use strawberry, but any flavour will work)

YOU WILL NEED

☐ Weighing scales

☐ 2 x 23cm round cake tins

☐ Non-stick baking parchment

☐ Electric hand-held mixer

☐ Spatula

☐ Palette knife

☐ Spoon

☐ Sieve

☐ Wooden spoon

HOW TO DO IT

1. Preheat the oven to 180°C/160°C fan/gas mark 4. Grease your 2 round tins, then line with a circle of non-stick baking parchment in the bottom and a strip around the side.

2. Put all the cake ingredients in a large mixing bowl, then beat together with an electric hand-held mixer for around 2 minutes, until the mixture is smooth, pale and creamy.

3. Pour half the cake mix into one prepared tin and the other half into the other tin. Gently smooth the tops with a spatula or palette knife, leaving a very small dip in the middle. (This is where the cake rises the most, and so this way you will have a flatter cake to decorate later.)

4. Ask an adult to put your cake tins in the preheated oven. Try to put them both on the middle shelf, so that they bake at the same time, but don't worry if you can't – just keep an eye on the higher one as it may be done a minute or two before the other. Bake for 30–35 minutes, until the cakes are lightly browned on top and feel springy to the touch.

5. While your cake bakes, make the buttercream. Beat the butter until smooth and creamy, using a wooden spoon or electric hand-held whisk, then sift in half the icing sugar and beat that in too.

6. When that is well mixed, sift in the other half of the icing sugar, along with the vanilla extract and milk.

7. Now it's time to beat, beat, beat! Do this for around 10 minutes, until your icing is pale, smooth and fluffy.

8. When an adult has helped you remove the cakes from the oven, leave them in their tins for 5 minutes, then turn them out onto wire racks to cool.

9. When the cakes are cool they are ready to fill. Get your serving plate or stand, and carefully place one of your cakes on top.

10. Use a spoon to blob the buttercream into the centre of the cake, then use a spatula or palette knife to smooth and spread it out to the edges of the cake.

11. Now spoon your jam over the butter icing and spread it very gently without dragging the buttercream.

12. Carefully place the other cake on top and dust with icing sugar.

   STORAGE: Can be stored in an airtight container somewhere cool for 3-4 days.

@ Try Something Different! @

Why not swap the vanilla extract in the cake and icing for the grated zest of a lemon? Then you can fill the cakes with lemon curd instead of jam and you'll have a luxurious lemon cake.

WHITE RABBIT CAKE

PREP TIME: 15 minutes **BAKE TIME:** 30-35 minutes

This is called White Rabbit Cake for a few reasons. First of all, it's a type of carrot cake, and everyone knows rabbits love carrots. But the real inspiration for this cake is the White Rabbit from 'Alice in Wonderland'. I like to imagine that Alice's poor little White Rabbit would be in less of a hurry if he was sitting with his feet up at the Mad Hatter's tea party enjoying a slice of his very own cake!

MAKES ONE 20CM SANDWICH SPONGE

FOR THE CAKE:

Unsalted butter, for greasing

350g **plain flour**, sifted

3 teaspoons **baking powder**

1 teaspoons **ground ginger**

½ teaspoons **ground nutmeg**

2 teaspoons **ground cinnamon**

300ml **sunflower oil**

400g **light soft brown sugar**

4 large free-range **eggs**

400g peeled and grated **carrot** (about 2 big or 3 small carrots)

FOR THE ICING:

400g **white chocolate**

150g **unsalted butter**

150ml **soured cream**

4 tablespoons **caster sugar**

White chocolate bunnies, to decorate

YOU WILL NEED

- ☐ Weighing scales
- ☐ 2 x 20cm round cake tins
- ☐ Non-stick baking parchment
- ☐ Grater
- ☐ Large mixing bowls
- ☐ Fork or small whisk
- ☐ Large metal spoon
- ☐ Small saucepan
- ☐ Heatproof bowl (that sits on top of the pan)
- ☐ Metal or bamboo skewer
- ☐ Whisk
- ☐ Wooden spoon
- ☐ Cooling rack
- ☐ Palette knife or spatula

1. Preheat the oven to 180°C/160° fan/gas mark 4. Grease your 2 round tins, and line them with a circle of non-stick baking parchment in the bottom and a strip around the side.

2. Put the flour, baking powder, ginger, nutmeg and cinnamon in a large mixing bowl.

3. In your other bowl, whisk together the oil, sugar and eggs. Stir in the grated carrot, then fold in the dry ingredients with a metal spoon. Pour half the cake mixture into one prepared cake tin and the other half into the other tin.

4. Ask an adult to put the tins in the preheated oven and bake for 30-35 minutes. Your cake is cooked when you put a skewer into the middle and it comes out clean. If the skewer has some mixture on it, leave for a further 5 minutes and check again.

5. While the cakes are in the oven, make your icing. Melt the white chocolate and butter in a heatproof bowl over a pan of gently simmering water, then leave to cool to room temperature.

6. When your chocolate mix is cool, put the soured cream into a small bowl and add the caster sugar. Whisk together until slightly fluffy, but be careful not to overmix. Now, add this to the chocolate and beat gently with a wooden spoon until combined. Put the bowl in the fridge for the icing to set a little.

7. When an adult has helped you remove the cakes from the oven, leave them in their tins for 5 minutes, then turn out onto wire racks to cool completely.

8. Now it's time to assemble your cake. Carefully place one of the cakes onto a serving plate and spread half the icing on top, using a palette knife or spatula. Place the second cake on top and spread the remaining icing over the top and around the sides – the easiest way to do this is to dollop plenty of icing on top of the cake, then push it over the sides and smooth the icing around with your palette knife or spatula. Add white chocolate bunnies on top to decorate, and serve.

STORAGE: Store this cake, covered, in the fridge (because of the soured cream icing) for up to 4 days. When you want a slice, leave the slice for 5 minutes out of the fridge to come to room temperature.

Cathryn Says:

This cake is brilliant for Easter or at your own Mad Hatter's tea party – or any time at all!

STICKY ST CLEMENTS' CAKE

PREP TIME: 1½ hours   **BAKE TIME:** 60 minutes

'Oranges and lemons say the bells of St Clements . . .' This sticky cake is juicy, sweet and zingy. You won't believe it, but the whole fruit, skin and all, is used. It's crazy but delicious! It's also made without flour and so it's great for anybody who is allergic to gluten.

MAKES ONE LARGE 23CM ROUND CAKE

Unsalted butter, for greasing

2 small unwaxed **oranges**

1 unwaxed **lemon**

120ml **water**

6 medium free-range **eggs**

275g **caster sugar**

275g **ground almonds**

1 teaspoon **baking powder** (check this is gluten free if that's what you want the cake to be)

Icing sugar, for dusting

YOU WILL NEED

- ☐ 1 x 23cm spring form tin
- ☐ Weighing scales
- ☐ Non-stick baking parchment
- ☐ Kitchen paper
- ☐ Small sharp knife
- ☐ Small saucepan with lid
- ☐ Sieve or colander
- ☐ Food processor (or electric hand-held mixer)
- ☐ Cooling rack

HOW TO DO IT

1. Grease your cake tin, then line it with a circle of non-stick baking parchment in the bottom and a strip around the side. Look out for the preheat the oven stage in Step 5. Wash your oranges and lemons well, then dry them with kitchen paper.

2. Ask an adult to help you cut the oranges into eighths and lemon into quarters. Remove any pips and the white pith from the middle of the fruit.

3. Put the fruit into a saucepan and pour the water over the fruit. Ask an adult to bring it to the boil, then turn the temperature right down, put a lid on the saucepan and simmer for 45 minutes. Ask an adult to keep checking on your pan – if the water gets very low, you might need to add an extra splash.

4. After 45 minutes, the fruit should be very soft and the water will have evaporated a bit. Ask an adult to take off the lid and leave it to simmer for another 5-10 minutes. Then turn off the heat and ask an adult to drain the water and tip the fruit into a bowl. Leave to cool for 10 minutes.

5. It's nearly time to put your cake in the oven, so preheat the oven to 190°C/170°C fan/gas mark 5.

6. Put the cooled fruit in a food processor and ask an adult to help you blitz until it is a bright, smooth purée. Add the remaining cake ingredients (except the icing sugar) and blitz again until you have a smooth batter.

7. Ask an adult to take the blade out of the food processor, then pour the mixture into your prepared tin and bake in the oven for 50–60 minutes, until the cake is springy to touch and a skewer comes out clean.

8. When an adult has helped you remove the cake from the oven, leave in the tin for 10 minutes, then turn out onto a wire rack to cool completely. Give your cake a generous dusting of icing sugar and it's ready to serve.

STORAGE: This cake is delicious with cream, or just on its own, and will keep in an airtight container for up to 7 days.

☆ Top Tip! ☆

If after around 40 minutes' baking, the top of your cake is going very dark, ask an adult to cover the the cake tin with some tin foil, which will stop the top from burning before the cake is fully cooked.

PANCAKE DAY... OR ANY DAY PANCAKES

PREP TIME: 10 minutes   **BAKE TIME:** 10 minutes

Pancakes are flippin' brilliant. I like mine best with lemon and sugar, but my little people like them with golden syrup and squirty cream. Making pancakes is amazingly quick and easy, so why should we only eat them on Pancake Day?

MAKES AROUND 12 PANCAKES (DEPENDING ON THE SIZE OF YOUR PAN)

100g **plain flour**, sifted

Pinch **salt**

2 medium free-range **eggs**, beaten

200ml **milk**, semi-skimmed or whole

50ml **water**

50g **unsalted butter**

YOU WILL NEED

- ☐ Large bowl
- ☐ Weighing scales
- ☐ Wooden spoon
- ☐ Measuring jug
- ☐ Electric hand-held mixer or balloon whisk
- ☐ Frying pan
- ☐ Small bowl
- ☐ Soup ladle or large spoon
- ☐ Fish slice or palette knife
- ☐ Silicone pastry brush or kitchen paper
- ☐ Plates

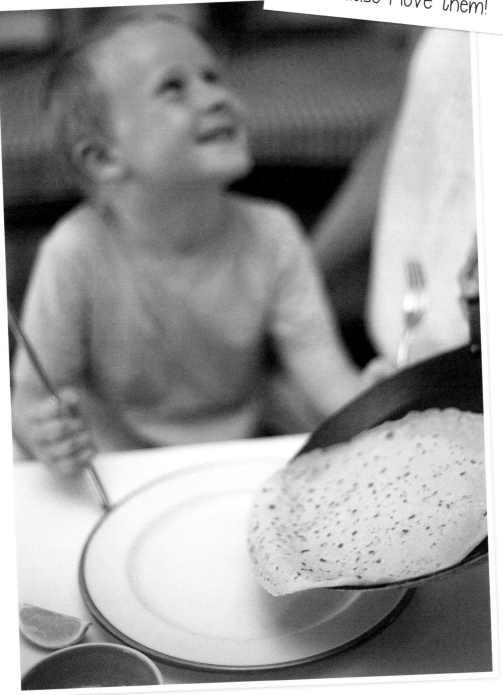

P.S. I know pancakes aren't technically baking, but I just couldn't leave this recipe out because I love them!

1. Put the flour and salt in a bowl and stir. Make a well in the centre of the flour and add the beaten eggs into it. Beat with an electric hand-held mixer or a whisk until combined.

2. In a jug, mix together the milk and water and add to the flour and eggs a little at a time, whisking continuously. Do this until all the liquid is used up and mixed in and you have a smooth, runny mixture. Don't panic if there are still some lumpy bits of flour – just keep whisking and they will soon disappear.

3. With the help of an adult, add the butter to the frying pan and melt over a medium heat. Pour 1 tablespoon of the butter into the pancake batter and whisk. Pour the rest into a small bowl and set aside.

4. Ask an adult to set the pan back over the heat. When it is nice and hot, it's time to start frying your pancakes – and flipping them, if you're brave enough! You will need an adult to help with all of this.

5. Use a soup ladle a little less than half full to add some batter to the pan. Don't add too much, you will need less than you think – these pancakes should be lovely and thin.

6. As soon as you pour the batter into the pan, gently tilt the pan so the mixture spreads out and covers the surface of the pan.

7. The pancake should take around 30–60 seconds to cook. Lift the edge with a spatula or palette knife to check if it's ready to flip. It should be lightly browned underneath. Flip the pancake over – with a palette knife, or a brave toss!

8. Cook the other side for about 15 seconds or so, then slide it out onto a plate and pass to whoever is first in the queue waiting to gobble it up. (This is what happens in our house!) Add more of the melted butter to the pan and cook the remaining pancakes in the same way.

STORAGE: Eat immediately.

Filling ideas

* Cream cheese, ground cinnamon and honey
* Nutella and chopped hazelnuts
* Black cherries and whipped cream
* Ice cream, strawberries and marshmallows
* Bananas and toffee sauce (see page 213)
* Blueberries and white chocolate chips

SWEETHEART SUGAR SHORTBREAD

PREP TIME: 10 minutes, plus 30 minutes chilling   **BAKE TIME:** 15 minutes

These simple shortbread biscuits are lovely. Eat them as a treat, share them with friends or make them as a special gift. They are perfect for your mum on Mother's Day, your grandma on her birthday or your best friend, just because.

MAKES AROUND 20–30 BISCUITS

200g **unsalted butter**, slightly soft

100g **golden caster sugar**, plus extra for sprinkling

300g **plain flour**, plus a little extra for dusting

Pinch of **salt**

YOU WILL NEED

- ☐ 1–2 baking trays
- ☐ Non-stick baking parchment
- ☐ Mixing bowl
- ☐ Wooden spoon or electric hand-held mixer
- ☐ Rolling pin
- ☐ Heart-shaped cutter (or any other sort of cutter)
- ☐ Cooling rack

1. Preheat the oven to 180°C/160°C/gas mark 4. Line 1–2 baking trays with non-stick baking parchment.

2. Cream together the butter and sugar in a big mixing bowl using a wooden spoon, or, if you have one, an electric hand-held mixer, until the mixture is smooth, pale and creamy.

3. Sift in the flour and salt, then beat the mixture until it begins to form a dough. Use your hands to bring it together, kneading gently until your dough is nice and smooth.

4. Lightly dust your worktop with flour, tip out the dough and roll it out with a rolling pin until it is about the thickness of two pound coins. Then cut out your hearts with your cookie cutter. Re-roll the trimmings to cut out more shapes if necessary.

5. When you have cut out all your biscuits, place them carefully onto your prepared baking tray. Ask an adult to help you put the tray in the oven and bake for 10-15 minutes, until they are a pale gold colour.

6. When an adult has removed the tray from the oven, sprinkle the hot biscuits with caster sugar, then carefully move to a wire rack to cool.

STORAGE: Store in an airtight container and eat within 5–7 days.

◎ Try Something Different! ◎

For a new flavour, add one of these at the end of Step 2 (before you add the flour and salt):

✱ 100g chocolate chips

✱ Grated zest of a lemon or orange

✱ 1 teaspoon vanilla extract

✱ 1 teaspoon mixed spice

✱ Dried lavender

✱ Freeze-dried strawberry pieces

✱ Chopped nuts

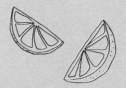

☆ Top Tip! ☆

Have a little pile of flour on a plate in which you can dip your cutter from time to time to stop it sticking.

SUMMER

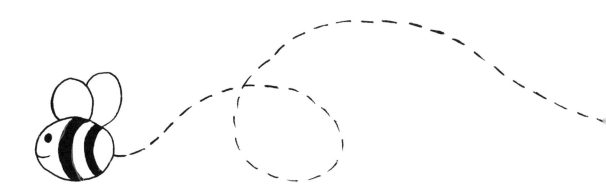

PERFECT PITTA POCKETS

PREP TIME: 1 hour   **BAKE TIME:** 10 minutes

These fabulous flatbreads are great for stuffing all your favourite things inside and enjoying for lunch or on a picnic. Cut into strips, they are perfect for dipping in your favourite dips too!

MAKES 8–10 PITTAS

500g **strong white flour**, plus a little extra for dusting

1 x 7g sachet of **fast-action yeast**

Large pinch of **salt**

300ml **warm water**

2 tablespoons **olive oil**, plus a little extra for greasing

YOU WILL NEED

☐ 2 large mixing bowls
☐ Weighing scales
☐ Cling film
☐ Measuring jug
☐ Baking tray
☐ Rolling pin

HOW TO DO IT

1. Lightly oil one of the large bowls ready for when your loaf needs to prove/ rise. Look out for the preheat the oven stage in Step 6.

2. Put the flour in your other large mixing bowl, then add the yeast on one side and the salt on the other. Make a well in the centre of the dry ingredients and pour in the water and oil.

3. Use one hand to start mixing the flour into the water and oil – just imagine your hand is a big spoon! Mix until all the ingredients have come together and you have a slightly sticky doughy mixture.

4. Lightly dust the worktop with flour, tip out the dough, then roll up your sleeves and start kneading. You'll need to do this for at least 15 minutes. You might need someone else to take turns with you, as it is hard work and your arms will be aching and ready to drop right off! After 15 minutes, you should have a smooth, stretchy soft ball of dough.

5. Put the dough in the lightly oiled mixing bowl and cover with cling film. Put this somewhere warm and leave to rise for 1–2 hours. By the time you return to your dough, it will have puffed up to double its size.

6. Now it's time to preheat the oven to 230°C/210°C fan/gas mark 7. Ask an adult to put the baking tray in the oven so that it warms as the oven heats up – it needs to be really hot before you put your pitta breads on it.

7. When the dough is ready, gently push out the air. Lightly dust your worktop with flour, divide the dough into 8–10 balls, then roll them out gently with a rolling pin to form small, flat, very thin pittas.

8. The oven and the baking tray will be really hot by now, so ask an adult to pull the tray out of the oven and arrange your pitta breads on it. It is best to bake just 2–3 pitta breads at a time because they puff up a lot! Bake for 5 minutes, but keep an eye on them. In the oven, the pitta breads will turn a pale gold colour and puff up like a balloon. They are ready as soon as they begin to deflate (as if they have popped).

9. Ask an adult to take them out of the oven, but be very careful, because the pitta breads will be filled with extremely hot steam. Repeat the instructions above to bake the rest of your dough.

10. When all your pitta breads have cooled a little, they are ready to be gobbled up! Fill them with any filling you fancy.

STORAGE: Any homemade bread is best eaten fresh on the day, but these will keep for 2–3 days wrapped in cling film.

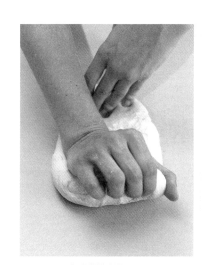

Our Favourite Fillings

✳ Hummus (see page 216), salad and grated carrot
✳ Tuna and cucumber
✳ Chicken, lettuce, tomato and guacamole
✳ Crispy bacon and cheddar cheese

EASY FETA CHEESE TRIANGLES

PREP TIME: 30 minutes   **BAKE TIME:** 20 minutes

These crispy cheesy pastry triangles are great for picnics, snacks or lunches.

MAKES 8 PARCELS

80ml **oil**, plus a little extra to grease the baking trays

A bunch of 8 or 9 **spring onions**, finely chopped (or snipped with scissors)

150g **frozen peas**

100g **ricotta cheese**

A handful of **fresh mint**, finely chopped

200g **feta cheese**

75g **unsalted butter**, melted

12 sheets **filo pastry**

Pinch of **salt** and **pepper**

YOU WILL NEED

- ☐ 2 baking trays
- ☐ Frying pan
- ☐ Weighing scales
- ☐ Wooden spoon
- ☐ Large bowl
- ☐ Kitchen paper
- ☐ Small saucepan
- ☐ Damp, clean tea towel
- ☐ Pastry brush
- ☐ Small sharp knife
- ☐ Dessertspoon

1. Preheat the oven to 200°C/180°C fan/gas mark 6. Lightly grease 2 baking trays.

2. Ask an adult to heat 1½ tablespoons of the oil in a frying pan over a medium heat. Add the spring onions and cook for 2 minutes. Add the frozen peas and stir them all around so that they start to defrost and go bright green. Tip into a large bowl and leave to cool for about 5 minutes.

3. Stir the ricotta into the pea mixture, add the mint and season with salt and pepper. Pat the feta dry with some kitchen paper and crumble into the mixture with your fingers. Stir together, and your filling is ready.

4. Ask an adult to help you melt the butter in a small saucepan, then mix in the rest of the oil and set aside.

5. Open the filo pastry and flatten it out on the worktop. Cover it with a damp, clean tea towel while you work to stop the pastry from drying out.

6. You need 3 sheets for each triangle. First, take 1 sheet and lay it on the worktop, brush with the oil and butter mix, then lay another sheet straight on top. Brush this sheet with the oil and butter, then lay the third sheet on top and brush again.

7. Ask an adult to help you to cut the pastry rectangle in half lengthways with a sharp knife, so you have two long rectangles.

8. Place 2 heaped dessertspoons of filling in one corner of the first strip of pastry. Gently lift the filled corner over diagonally and fold tightly to make a triangle shape. Continue to lift and fold, keeping the triangle shape, to the end of the pastry. You should now have a neat triangle parcel. Do the same with the other piece of layered pastry.

9. Repeat the layering, filling and folding until you have used up all the pastry sheets and filling. You should now have 8 triangle parcels.

10. Put the triangles onto their prepared baking trays and brush each one with the remaining butter.

11. Ask an adult to put them in the preheated oven and bake for 15–20 minutes until the pastry is golden brown.

STORAGE: Store in an an airtight container in the fridge and eat within 3 days.

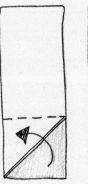  

SUNSHINE FRITTATA

PREP TIME: 20 minutes **BAKE TIME:** 15 minutes

This is a lovely, easy recipe that looks and tastes like a warm plate of sunshine.

MAKES 1 LARGE FRITTATA IN A PAN

3 **sweet potatoes** (about 400g), peeled and thinly sliced

8 large free-range **eggs**, beaten

Pinch of **salt** and **pepper**

½ teaspoon **smoked paprika** (optional)

1 tablespoon **oil**

½ **red onion,** very thinly sliced (optional)

1 **red pepper**, deseeded and chopped into small slices

150g **soft goat's cheese**, crumbled

YOU WILL NEED
- ☐ Saucepan
- ☐ Weighing scales
- ☐ Colander or sieve
- ☐ Mixing bowl
- ☐ Medium-large ovenproof frying pan
- ☐ Wooden spoon

HOW TO DO IT

1. Preheat the oven to 200°C/180°C/gas mark 6.

2. Ask an adult to bring a saucepan of water to the boil and help you drop in the sweet potato. Cook for 6 minutes, then drain and set aside.

3. In a bowl, mix the eggs with the paprika, if using, and season with salt and pepper.

4. Ask an adult to help you heat half the oil in a large ovenproof frying pan over medium heat and fry the onion and pepper for 5 minutes. Add these to the egg mixture and stir. Then stir in the potatoes.

5. Add the remaining oil to the frying pan and tip in the egg mixture. Turn the heat down to low and cook for 5 minutes – the base of the frittata will start to cook and set.

6. Carefully arrange the cheese on top, then ask an adult to put the pan in the oven to bake for 10-15 minutes, until cooked through.

STORAGE: Enjoy hot or cold on the day you make it. If you are going to eat it cold later, just turn it out of its pan and store in the fridge for up to 3 days.

ANY-WAY-YOU-WANT-IT PIZZA

PREP TIME: 30 minutes, plus 1 hour proving/rising

BAKE TIME: 25 minutes

Pizza is a firm favourite in our house. Once the dough is ready, it is such a quick and fun thing to make together. Keep your topping simple with cheese and tomato, or be more creative. It's up to you - any way you want it!

MAKES 2 MEDIUM OR 4 SMALL PIZZAS

FOR THE BASE(S):

300g **strong white flour**, plus a little extra for dusting

1 x 7g sachet of **fast-action yeast**

225ml **warm water**

1 teaspoon **salt**

4 tablespoons **olive oil**

FOR THE TOPPING:

A small drop of **olive oil**

1 **garlic clove**, very finely chopped and crushed with the side of the knife

150ml **passata**

1 teaspoon **dried oregano**

1 teaspoon **caster sugar**

Pinch of **salt** and **pepper**

125g **buffalo mozzarella**

YOU WILL NEED

- ☐ 2 large mixing bowls
- ☐ Weighing scales
- ☐ 2 baking trays
- ☐ Cling film
- ☐ Measuring jug
- ☐ Small saucepan
- ☐ Wooden spoon
- ☐ Rolling pin

Our Favourite Toppings

For 'The Ambrose'
1 ball of mozzarella, sliced or torn
1 handful of grated Parmesan cheese
8-10 slices of thinly sliced chorizo

For 'The Maisie'
60g smoked salmon, torn into pieces
2 cooked new potatoes, thinly sliced
75g cream cheese, spooned onto the
pizza in blobs

Other Topping Ideas

✳ Roast chicken and sweetcorn
✳ Ham and mushroom
✳ Goat's cheese and peppers
✳ Sausage and bacon

1. You will need a large bowl and cling film ready for when your loaf needs to prove/rise. Lightly oil one of the large bowls and the baking trays ready for use. Look out for the preheat the oven stage in Step 7.

2. Begin by making your pizza base. Put the flour in a large mixing bowl, then add the yeast on one side and the salt on the other. Make a well in the centre of the dry ingredients and pour in three-quarters of the water and oil.

3. Use one hand, start mixing the flour into the water and oil – just imagine your hand is a big spoon! Mix until all the ingredients have come together and you have a slightly sticky doughy mixture.

4. Lightly dust the worktop with flour, tip out the dough, then roll up your sleeves and start kneading. You'll need to do this for at least 15 minutes. You might need someone else to take turns with you, as it is hard work and your arms will be aching and ready to drop right off! After 15 minutes, you should have a smooth, stretchy and soft ball of dough.

5. Put the dough in the greased bowl, cover with cling film and put it in a warm place to double in size for around 1 hour.

6. Meanwhile, make your super speedy sauce. Ask an adult to help you to heat a little oil in a saucepan over a medium heat and fry the garlic for 1 minute. Pour in the passata and stir, then add the oregano, sugar and seasoning. Leave to cook over a low heat for about 10 minutes, then set aside.

7. When the dough has risen, tip it out onto the worktop and gently bring it back together to a neat ball. Divide into 2 pieces (or 4 if you're making smaller pizzas). Now, preheat the oven to 230°C/210°C/gas mark 8.

8. Roll out each ball of dough into large, thin rounds and place them on the prepared baking trays. Now spread over the sauce and add your mozzarella, plus any other toppings.

9. Ask an adult to put the trays in the oven and bake for about 25 minutes, by which time the base should be golden and crisp and the toppings perfectly cooked.

STORAGE: Eat straight away.

☆ Top Tip! ☆

Pizza dough should be quite sticky and wetter than for a white loaf, but if it is too sticky to knead, you can add a little extra flour on the worktop and knead it into the dough – just be careful not to add too much.

TEENY TOMATO PESTO BITES

PREP TIME: 10 minutes   **BAKE TIME:** 10-12 minutes

These teeny bites of loveliness couldn't be quicker. Cut, blob, dot and bake . . . and ta-dah! They're brilliant for parties or you can pop them in a container and add them to your picnic basket.

MAKES ABOUT 48 BITES

1 x 375g pack of shop-bought ready-rolled **puff pastry**

Plain flour, for dusting

1 medium free-range **egg**, beaten

100g **pesto**

200g **cherry tomatoes**, halved

Handful of **fresh basil**, to decorate (optional)

YOU WILL NEED

☐ Baking tray
☐ Parchment paper
☐ Weighing scales
☐ Sharp knife
☐ Pastry brush
☐ Teaspoon

HOW TO DO IT

1. Preheat the oven to 200°C/180°C fan/gas mark 6. Line a baking tray with non-stick baking parchment.

2. Lightly dust the worktop with flour, then lay the sheet of puff pastry on top and ask an adult to help you cut it into squares around 3 x 3cm big (about half the size of a playing card).

3. Put the pastry squares on the prepared baking tray, leaving small spaces between them, and brush with the beaten egg.

4. Using a teaspoon, push a little round dent into the middle of each square. Be careful not to push a hole in the pastry though!

5. Now, with your teaspoon, put a small dollop of pesto in the little dent and top each pesto blob with a halved tomato, flat side up.

6. Ask an adult to put your bites into the preheated oven and bake for 10–12 minutes. Top with the fresh basil once cooked, if using.

STORAGE: Enjoy hot or cold, store in an airtight container in the fridge and eat within 5 days.

NANNY'S RASPBERRY CREAM SLICES

PREP TIME: 20 minutes **BAKE TIME:** 25 minutes

Who can resist a cream cake? Not me, that's for sure, and not my mum either. Perfect to enjoy on sunny days at the seaside, or in the garden.

I would like to dedicate this recipe to my lovely mum – she is amazing!

MAKES 18 SLICES

2 x 375g packs of shop-bought ready-rolled **puff pastry**

400ml **double cream**

175g **icing sugar**, plus 2 tablespoons

1 medium free-range **egg**, beaten

1 teaspoon **vanilla extract**

4 tablespoons **raspberry jam**

About 4 tablespoons **water**

A drop of **pink food colour**

300g **fresh raspberries**, halved

YOU WILL NEED

- ☐ 2 baking trays (you will need to cook in 2 batches)
- ☐ Non-stick baking parchment
- ☐ Weighing scales
- ☐ Fork
- ☐ Cooling rack
- ☐ 2 large mixing bowls
- ☐ Balloon whisk
- ☐ Sieve
- ☐ Chopping board
- ☐ Large sharp knife
- ☐ Spatula or palette knife
- ☐ Spoon or piping bag and nozzle (optional)

1. Preheat the oven to 200°C/180°C fan/gas mark 6. Line 1 of your baking trays with non-stick baking parchment.

2. Put one sheet of pastry on top of your lined baking tray, then prick the pastry all over with a fork. Place the other baking tray on top – this will stop the pastry puffing up too much.

3. Ask an adult to put your pastry tray in the oven and bake for 15 minutes. After this time, an adult can remove the top tray. Brush with egg and sprinkle with 1 tablespoon of icing sugar. Bake for another 10 minutes, then remove the tray from the oven and put on a wire rack to cool completely. Repeat with the other pastry sheet.

4. Now make the vanilla cream. Put the cream in a large mixing bowl, sift over 40g of the icing sugar and add the vanilla. Use a whisk or an electric hand-held mixer to beat the cream until thick. Chill in the fridge until you are ready to use.

5. When the pastry has cooled, put the first sheet onto a large chopping board and spread the raspberry jam all over. Slice this sheet into 18 rectangles and set aside.

6. Sift the remaining icing sugar into a bowl and add enough water to make a thick icing. Add a tiny drop of pink food colouring to the remaining icing and mix.

7. Cut the second pastry sheet into 18 rectangles, as before. Then drizzle or pipe the pink icing over the iced sheet.

8. Now, dollop the whipped cream on to each jam-covered slice and spread to leave a thick covering.

9. Lay some halved fresh raspberries on top of the cream, then a few small dots of cream (to act as glue), then top with a pretty iced lid. Repeat with all 9 and you will have a collection of irresistible, enormous cream slices . . . delicious!

STORAGE: Store in the fridge and eat within 2-3 days.

Cathryn Says:

This is a recipe inspired by the delicious - and truly enormous! - cream cakes at our favourite café by the sea.

FRIENDSHIP CHAIN CAKE

This is the perfect cake to start at the beginning of the summer holidays. It's based on a sourdough batter, and your job is to grow, feed and look after it, in order to make a yummy cake at the end. When you've started your batter, you give away a quarter of the mixture each to three of your friends. They look after their share of cake batter too and divide it up, share it out and keep one quarter to bake their own cake.

Just imagine how far the friendship chain could go, and how many people you could inspire to bake!

MAKES 1 CAKE (PLUS ENOUGH BATTER TO GIVE TO 3 FRIENDS)

200g **wholemeal flour**
150g **caster sugar**
300ml **whole milk**
50ml **water**
1 tablespoon **dried yeast** (not fast-action)

YOU WILL NEED
- ☐ Large mixing bowl
- ☐ Weighing scales
- ☐ Wooden spoon
- ☐ Small saucepan
- ☐ Small mixing bowl
- ☐ Cling film
- ☐ Balloon whisk
- ☐ Clean tea towel
- ☐ 4 containers or bowls (large ice cream tubs will do)

STEP 1
YOUR CAKE STARTER MIXTURE

PREP TIME: 15 minutes   **BAKE TIME:** 50 minutes

HOW TO DO IT

1. Put the flour and sugar in a large mixing bowl and stir together.

2. Ask an adult to help you heat the milk and water in a small saucepan over medium heat for 2–3 minutes. Take off the heat and pour into another small mixing bowl.

3. Mix the yeast into the milk and water, then cover the bowl with cling film and leave for 10 minutes.

4. When the 10 minutes are up, whisk the yeast mixture into the flour, then cover the bowl with a clean tea towel and leave on the worktop for 24 hours.

5. After 24 hours, ask an adult to help you divide the mixture into 4 separate bowls or containers.

NOW . . . Choose 3 lucky friends. Give 3 bowls or containers away to your friends with the instructions on the next page. You will need to follow the instructions too with the quarter of the mix you keep for yourself.

STEP 2
GROW YOUR BATTER

These are the instructions for you and your friends to follow:

FOR FEEDING THE MIX

300g plain flour
400g caster sugar
480ml milk

YOU WILL NEED

☐ Large mixing bowl
☐ Weighing scales
☐ Clean tea towel
☐ Wooden spoon
☐ 4 containers or bowls (ice cream tubs will do)

I am your very own Friendship Chain Cake Starter. I am alive and need looking after. I need to sit on your worktop for 10 days without a lid on, and away from draughts so I don't get too cold. Please don't put me in the fridge or I will fall asleep, like a hibernating bear. If I stop bubbling, I am too sleepy to keep.

DAY 1: Put your cake batter into a large mixing bowl and cover loosely with a clean tea towel.

DAY 2: Stir well

DAY 3: Stir well

DAY 4: Feed your cake mix. Add half the plain flour, half the caster sugar and half the milk. Stir well.

DAY 5: Stir well

DAY 6: Stir well

DAY 7: Stir well

DAY 8: Stir well

DAY 9: Add the remaining ingredients and stir well. Divide the batter into 4 equal portions. Keep 1 portion for yourself and give the other 3 to 3 more friends, along with a copy of the instructions. Keep your mix covered with a clean tea towel until tomorrow, when you can bake with it.

DAY 10: Hooray – you are ready to make your cake!

DAY 1

STIR WELL

FEED YOUR CAKE MIX

DAY 9

STEP 3
BAKE YOUR FRIENDSHIP CHAIN CAKE

PREP TIME: 20 minutes **BAKE TIME:** 50 minutes

Now it's time to transform your cake batter into a delicious sponge cake by adding just a few ingredients.

MAKES 1 MEDIUM CAKE

50g **unsalted butter**, plus a little extra for greasing

2 **cooking apples**, peeled, cored and chopped into small cubes

200g **caster sugar**

300g **plain flour**

Pinch of **salt**

2 teaspoons **baking powder**

2 medium free-range **eggs**, beaten

2 teaspoons **vanilla extract**

1 teaspoon **ground cinnamon**

100g **dried blueberries**

100g **fresh blueberries**

50g **Demerara sugar**

YOU WILL NEED

☐ 23cm cake tin or silicone mould
☐ Non-stick baking parchment (if using metal cake tin)
☐ Weighing scales
☐ Small saucepan
☐ Large mixing bowl
☐ Wooden spoon
☐ Cooling rack

1. Preheat the oven to 180°C/160°C fan/gas mark 6. Grease and line the cake tin with non-stick baking parchment.

2. Ask an adult to help you melt the butter in a small saucepan over a low heat, then add this to your cake batter, along with all the other ingredients except for the Demerara sugar and the fresh blueberries. Mix until well combined. Then add the blueberries and stir.

3. Pour the mixture into your prepared cake tin and sprinkle the Demerara sugar over the top.

4. Ask an adult to put the cake in the oven and bake for 45–50 minutes until golden and springy to the touch. If you test the middle with a skewer, it should come out clean. If not, put it back in the oven for a couple more minutes.

5. Leave the cake in the tin for 5 minutes to cool, then turn out on to a wire rack to cool completely.

STORAGE: The baked cake will keep for up to 7 days in an airtight container.

Enjoying Your Cake

This is lovely served warm
with ice cream, or wrapped in foil
and taken out on adventures to be
eaten along the way.
Why not get together with the
friends you shared the mix with?
You can try each other's and
decide whose is best!

MALTY MOON CUSTARD BISCUITS

PREP TIME: 15 minutes   **BAKE TIME:** 8-10 minutes

These moon-shaped biscuits are a cross between a custard cream and a malted milk, two of my favourite biscuits. They are ideal to bake at a sleepover with friends. And they'll be ready just in time to enjoy for your midnight feast!

MAKES ABOUT 20 SANDWICHED BISCUITS

FOR THE BISCUITS:

200g **plain flour,** plus a little extra for dusting

50g **custard powder**

50g **malted drink powder,** such as Horlicks

25g **icing sugar**

175g **unsalted butter,** cut into cubes

FOR THE FILLING:

50g **unsalted butter,** soft

150g **icing sugar**

1 tablespoon **custard powder**

1 tablespoon **malted drink powder**

1 tablespoon **full-fat milk**

YOU WILL NEED

- ☐ 2 baking trays
- ☐ Non-stick baking parchment
- ☐ Food processor
- ☐ Cling film
- ☐ Mixing bowl
- ☐ Wooden spoon (or an electric hand-held mixer)
- ☐ Sieve
- ☐ Rolling pin
- ☐ Moon-shaped cutter (or another shape if you prefer)
- ☐ Cooling rack
- ☐ Teaspoon

1. Preheat the oven to 180°C/160°C fan/gas mark 4. Line 2 baking trays with non-stick baking parchment.

2. Put the flour, custard powder, malted drink powder and icing sugar in a food processor and pulse until all the ingredients are mixed. Add the butter and pulse again until it starts to come together and form a dough.

3. Ask an adult to remove the blade from the processor and bring the dough together with your hands. Flatten the dough into a disc, wrap in cling film and chill in the fridge for around 15–20 minutes.

4. Now make the filling. Beat the butter until soft, using a wooden spoon or an electric hand-held mixer, then sift the icing sugar, custard powder and malted drink powder into the bowl and beat again. Add the milk and give it one last beat until you have a smooth, creamy, but slightly stiff mix.

5. Take the chilled dough out of the fridge, unwrap and divide it in half – this makes it easier to roll. Lightly dust your worktop with flour and, using a rolling pin, roll out one half of the dough until it is a little thicker than a pound coin.

6. Use your cookie cutter to cut out your shapes and put them on the lined baking tray. Put in the fridge while you roll out the other half of the dough to keep it chilled. When you have cut out and laid the second half of the biscuits on your other baking tray, put them in the fridge with the others for 5 minutes.

7. Ask an adult to help you put the baking trays in the oven and bake for 8-10 minutes until they are a pale golden colour. Place on a wire rack to cool.

8. When your biscuits are completely cool, it's time to do the filling. Use a teaspoon to put a little dollop of icing on one of your biscuits, then place another biscuit on top, like a sandwich. Repeat until you have used up all the biscuits.

STORAGE: Store in an airtight container and eat within 5 days.

☆ Top Tip! ☆
If you don't have a food processor, just cream together the butter and icing sugar, then sift in the other ingredients and stir until it comes together.

☆ Top Tip! ☆
Make sure you have an even number of biscuits, so that you don't have leftover halves when you make your sandwiches!

QUEEN OF HEARTS' TARTS

♡ ♡

PREP TIME: 30 minutes **BAKE TIME:** 10 -12 minutes

Sometimes simple is just the thing, and this recipe is exactly that. Lovely pastry and sticky strawberry jam. A perfect summer treat.

MAKES 12 TARTS

FOR THE PASTRY:

75g **unsalted butter**, cold, cut into small cubes, plus a little extra for greasing

150g **plain flour**, plus a little extra for dusting

Grated zest of ½ an **orange** (optional)

2–3 tablespoons **juice from the zested orange**

FOR THE FILLING:

About 200g **strawberry jam**

YOU WILL NEED

☐ 12-hole tart tin (not a deep muffin tin)
☐ Weighing scales
☐ Mixing bowl
☐ Metal table knife
☐ Cling film
☐ Rolling pin
☐ Round pastry cutter
☐ Spoon
☐ Cooling rack

HOW TO DO IT

1. Preheat the oven to 180°C/160°C fan/gas mark 4. Lightly grease the 12-hole tart tin with butter.

2. Put the flour in a bowl and stir in the orange zest, if using. Add the cubed butter and use your fingertips to break up and rub in the butter until the mixture looks like breadcrumbs.

3. Pour the water into the flour and use a table knife to cut through and stir the mixture until it begins to form a ball of dough. Bring together with your hands, flatten into a disc and wrap in cling film. Chill in the fridge for 20 minutes.

4. Roll the pastry out on a lightly dusted worktop to just slightly thicker than a pound coin. Use your cutter to cut out 12 discs, a little bigger than the holes in your tin.

5. Gently press a pastry disc into each hole in the tin and spoon a generous teaspoon of jam into each pastry case.

6. Ask an adult to help you to put the tray in the preheated oven and bake for 10-12 minutes. Let them cool for 5 minutes before asking an adult to remove them from the tin and transfer to a wire rack to cool completely.

STORAGE: Store in an airtight container and eat within 5 days.

Cathryn Says:

Enjoy as a little afternoon tea or take them on a picnic – but watch out for that naughty Knave of Hearts (and everyone else) who'll want to steal them!

TERRIFIC TIFFIN

PREP TIME: 15 minutes **CHILL TIME:** 1-2 hours

Not strictly baking, but this is such a terrific chocolatey treat I couldn't resist including it. Put a few into a little gift bag, tie with ribbon and add a homemade label to make the perfect gift – for birthdays, Father's Day, or even a teacher's end of term present.

MAKES 12 PIECES

100g **unsalted butter**, plus a little extra for greasing

200g **digestive biscuits**

150g **milk chocolate**, broken into pieces or chopped

150g **dark chocolate**, broken into pieces or chopped

150g **golden syrup**

100g **dried apricots**, chopped

75g **raisins**

75g **glacé cherries**, chopped

YOU WILL NEED

- ☐ 20cm square tin
- ☐ Non-stick baking parchment
- ☐ Weighing scales
- ☐ Cling film
- ☐ Freezer bag and rolling pin (optional)
- ☐ Medium/large mixing bowl
- ☐ Saucepan
- ☐ Heatproof bowl (that will sit on top of the pan)
- ☐ Wooden spoon or spatula
- ☐ Chopping board
- ☐ Sharp knife

HOW TO DO IT

1. Grease the inside of your tin with butter, then line with cling film or non-stick baking parchment (leaving some overhanging the edges of the tin).

2. Break up the biscuits into little pieces. The most fun way to do this is to put them all in a plastic freezer or sandwich bag and use the end of a rolling pin to bash them. Or you could just break them with your hands. Put the dried fruit and broken biscuits in your mixing bowl.

3. Put both types of chocolate, the butter and the syrup into a heatproof bowl that is big enough to sit on top of a saucepan.

4. Fill the saucepan with water and ask an adult to set it over a medium-high heat and bring to the boil. Turn it down so it is just simmering, then place the bowl on top (make sure the water does not touch the base of the bowl) and let the chocolate, butter and syrup melt together. Remove the bowl from the heat and pour the melted chocolate over the biscuits and fruit and stir together until everything is covered in chocolate.

5. Now, tip your mixture into the prepared tin. Spread it out evenly using the back of a spoon or a spatula and leave to cool for a few minutes. Transfer to the fridge to set for 1-2 hours.

6. When your tiffin has set, turn it out of the tin onto a chopping board, remove the cling film, and ask an adult to help you cut it into 12 squares. Share and enjoy!

STORAGE: If the weather is hot, you will need to keep your tiffin in the fridge. Otherwise, keep it in an airtight container for up to 7 days.

◎ Try Something Different! ◎

Why not experiment with the recipe? Try adding nuts, different fruit, different biscuits or even chopped up chocolate bars.

☆ Top Tip! ☆

Drizzle melted white chocolate over the top of the finished tiffin for a double chocolate treat.

HONEY BEE BISCUITS

PREP TIME: 20 minutes **BAKE TIME:** 8-10 minutes

These biscuits are buttery and crunchy with a delicious taste of honey. They are perfect for busy little bees – in lunchboxes, picnics or as a teatime treat. You can leave them plain or decorate them with little fondant bees.

MAKES ABOUT 30 BISCUITS

125g **unsalted butter**, at room temperature

65g **icing sugar**

1 tablespoon **honey**

1 large free-range **egg white**

150g **plain flour**, plus a little extra for dusting

Pinch of **salt**

50g **Demerara sugar**, for rolling the dough in

FOR THE DECORATION YOU WILL NEED

☐ 10g each of **yellow and black fondant icing**

☐ A few **flaked almonds**

☐ 1 teaspoon **honey** or **water** and a paintbrush to stick the decorations to the biscuits

☐ Rolling pin

☐ Paint/pastry brush

YOU WILL NEED

☐ Baking tray

☐ Non-stick baking parchment

☐ Large mixing bowl

☐ Electric hand-held mixer or wooden spoon

☐ Cling film

☐ Weighing scales

☐ Sharp knife

☐ Cooling rack

HOW TO DO IT

1. Line a baking tray with non-stick baking parchment. Look out for the preheat the oven stage in Step 4.

2. Beat the butter and icing sugar together in a large mixing bowl until they are pale and creamy. You can do this with an electric hand-held mixer or a wooden spoon. Add the honey and beat a little more, then add the egg white and beat again. Add the flour and salt to the mixture and stir gently until it comes together to form a dough.

3. Dust your hands with a little flour and very lightly dust the worktop too. Tip out the dough and form into a ball, then roll into a long sausage shape, about the size of a rolling pin (about 30cm long and 5cm wide). Sprinkle the Demerara sugar over the dough and on the worktop. Roll the dough in the sugar until it is covered in a sugary coating.

4. Cut the dough in half and wrap both halves in cling film, then put in the fridge to chill for about 1 hour. Preheat the oven to 180°C/160°C fan/gas mark 4.

5. Take the dough out of the fridge and unwrap it. Ask an adult to help cut the dough into discs about as thick as 2 pound coins. Place the biscuits on your prepared baking tray, leaving small gaps between each biscuit.

6. Ask an adult to help you to put the baking tray into the oven and bake for 8-10 minutes. They should still be pale but firm to touch. Leave to cool on the tray for 5 minutes, then transfer to a wire rack to cool completely. When the biscuits are cool, you can decorate them however you like.

STORAGE: Fondant icing decorations can sweat in airtight containers so only decorate the ones you are going to use and eat, otherwise store the un-iced biscuits in your container and use within 5 days.

BUZZY BEE DECORATION

Roll little ovals of yellow fondant icing, then roll thin black stripes to lie over the top. Finally, stick in flaked almonds as wings.

OR

Roll thin lengths of yellow and black fondant icing, line them up side by side and then roll over them with a rolling pin. You will have a bee-striped icing which can be cut into small discs and stuck on top of the biscuits with a little honey or water.

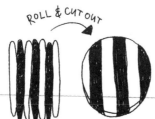

ROLL & CUT OUT

  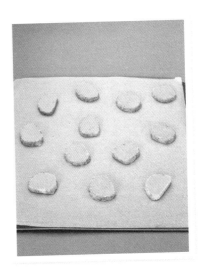

SCRUMPTIOUS STRAWBERRY AND CREAM MERINGUES

PREP TIME: 20 minutes   **BAKE TIME:** 1½ hours

The best meringues are crispy on the outside and chewy inside. Meringues are one of my favourite treats and these are filled with strawberries and cream – one of the loveliest tastes of English summertime.

MAKES ABOUT 15 MERINGUES

4 large free-range **egg whites** (at room temperature)

150g **caster sugar**

75g **icing sugar**

300ml **clotted cream**

300g **fresh strawberries**, thinly sliced

YOU WILL NEED

- ☐ 2 baking trays
- ☐ Non-stick baking parchment (or reusable silicone baking paper)
- ☐ Large, very clean, metal mixing bowl
- ☐ Weighing scales
- ☐ Electric hand-held mixer
- ☐ Sieve
- ☐ Large metal spoon
- ☐ 2 dessertspoons
- ☐ Cooling rack
- ☐ Palette knife
- ☐ Small sharp knife

1. Preheat the oven to 110°C/90°C/gas mark ¼. Line 2 baking trays with non-stick baking parchment.

2. Tip the egg whites into a very clean metal bowl and use an electric hand-held mixer to beat them. At first, big bubbles will appear and the eggs will go frothy, but slowly the bubbles will get smaller and the mixture will turn white and become stiffer.

3. Now you are ready to start adding the caster sugar. Keep beating the egg whites as you add the sugar a tablespoon at a time, beating the mixture between each spoonful. When you have added all the sugar, the mixture will be thick and shiny and should stand up in little peaks when you lift up your whisk.

4. Gently sift the icing sugar over the mixture and fold through with a large clean metal spoon. Be careful not to over mix the meringue or knock the air out of it by folding too much or too hard. When you have finished, the mixture will be soft and look like a big fluffy cloud.

5. Use 2 dessertspoons to shape the meringues. Scoop up a big spoonful of meringue with one spoon, and use the other to push the mixture off onto your prepared baking tray. Repeat until you have used all your meringue mixture, leaving a small space between each meringue.

6. Ask an adult to help you put your meringues in the oven and bake for 1½ hours. After this time, the meringues should be crisp on the outside and a very pale brown colour (like the colour of very milky coffee). Ask an adult to remove your meringues from the oven and leave them to cool completely on their trays.

7. When you want to serve, gently spread a spoonful of clotted cream onto the base of one meringue, then layer some sliced strawberries on top. Add a little tiny extra blob of cream to the base of another meringue and sandwich together.

STORAGE: Store (unfilled) in an airtight container and eat within 4-5 days. Any filled meringues can be stored in the fridge for a day or two but the meringue will become a little wet and not as crisp.

Cathryn Says:

Why not pick your own strawberries? Going strawberry picking is one of our favourite summer activities; late June is usually the best time to go.

◎ Try Something Different! ◎

For a Summer Strawberry Mess, just crush up the meringues and mix with strawberries and whipped cream.

WICKED CHOCOLATE BROWNIES

PREP TIME: 15 minutes **BAKE TIME:** 35-40 minutes

Almost everyone loves a chocolate brownie, so here is my easy recipe for rich, gooey, totally wicked brownies.

MAKES 9 SQUARES

125g **unsalted butter**, soft, plus a little extra for greasing

100g **dark chocolate**, finely chopped

275g **caster sugar**

½ teaspoon **vanilla extract**

2 large free-range **eggs**, lightly beaten

50g **self-raising flour**

25g **plain flour**

2 tablespoons **cocoa powder**

YOU WILL NEED

☐ 1 x 25cm x 17cm approx traybake tin
☐ Non-stick baking parchment
☐ Heatproof bowl
☐ Weighing scales
☐ Small saucepan
☐ Wooden spoon or electric hand-held mixer
☐ Large mixing bowl
☐ Sharp knife
☐ Spoon or spatula

1. Preheat the oven 180°C/160°C fan/gas mark 4. Grease your tin with a little butter or oil, then line with non-stick baking parchment.

2. Put the chopped chocolate in a heatproof bowl and melt over a pan of simmering water with the help of an adult. Take it off the heat and set aside.

3. Beat the butter, sugar and vanilla together in a large mixing bowl until creamy and fluffy. The add the eggs, a little at a time, beating between each addition. Add both types of flour and the cocoa into the butter, sugar and egg mixture, then pour in the melted chocolate too and stir until it is all combined.

4. Tip the mix into your prepared tin and use the back of a spoon or a spatula to make sure it's nice and even. Ask an adult to put the tray into the oven and bake for 35-40 minutes. When the brownie is ready, a light, crackly crust will have formed on top and it will have risen very slightly. It will still be soft in the middle – and this is right.

5. Leave in the tin for about 20 minutes, then ask an adult to help cut it into squares and carefully remove it from the tin. Enjoy!

STORAGE: Store in an airtight container and eat within 5 days.

Cathryn Says:
I can't resist eating these when they are still a tiny bit warm, but they are also extra fudgy and delicious the next day too.

AUTUMN

SPICY CHICKEN FILO ROLLS WITH MANGO CHUTNEY

PREP TIME: 30 minutes   **BAKE TIME:** 25 minutes

These lightly-spiced crispy rolls are a perfect savoury snack. They are totally irresistible dipped in sticky, sweet mango chutney.

MAKES 8 ROLLS

2 medium **potatoes**, peeled, cooked and cut into cubes

75ml **oil**

1 small **onion**, finely chopped

4 skinless and boneless **chicken thighs**, cut into smartie-sized pieces

2 tablespoons **mild curry paste**

3 tablespoons **Greek yogurt**

50g baby **spinach**

Small handful of fresh **coriander**, chopped

8 sheets of **filo pastry**

1 x good-quality jar of **mango chutney**, for dipping

YOU WILL NEED

- ☐ Baking tray
- ☐ Weighing scales
- ☐ Large frying pan
- ☐ Wooden spoon
- ☐ Fork
- ☐ Small bowl
- ☐ Tea towel
- ☐ Pastry brush

1. Lightly grease a baking tray. Preheat the oven to 200°C/180°C/gas mark 6.

2. Ask an adult to help you heat 1 tablespoon of oil in a frying pan and fry the onion for a few minutes until soft. Add the chicken and stir around the pan for about 5 minutes until golden and cooked through.

3. Add the curry paste and stir into the onion and chicken. Cook for 2 minutes, then turn down the heat and stir in the yogurt.

4. Use a fork to crush the cooked potatoes a little in a bowl, then stir these into the mixture. Finally, add the spinach and coriander and continue to cook until the spinach has wilted. Tip the mixture into a bowl and set aside to cool.

5. Unwrap the filo pastry, lay it flat on the worktop and cover with a damp tea towel (to stop it drying out). Take the first sheet of pastry and put it in front of you with the short side closest to you. Put 3 tablespoons of filling in a line along the short end of the pastry closest to you, leaving a 3–4cm border around the filling.

6. Use a pastry brush to brush all the pastry you can see with oil. Fold either side of the pastry in towards the middle to almost meet each other over the filling. And again, brush over all the pastry you can see with some of the oil.

7. Roll up the pastry away from you until you have a neatly sealed roll. Repeat until you have used all of the pastry sheets and filling. You should now have 8 filo rolls ready for the oven.

8. Place your filo rolls onto the baking tray, then brush with a little more of the oil. With the help of an adult, put into the oven to bake for 25 minutes, until crisp and golden.

9. Put your sticky chutney in a pot or bowl ready to dip the hot spicy chicken rolls into – and enjoy!

STORAGE: These are most delicious warm, but can easily be kept in the fridge and eaten cold, maybe in your lunchbox. Eat within 2 days.

☆ Top Tip! ☆

The filling can be made in advance and kept in the fridge until you are ready to make and bake your tasty chicken rolls.

◎ Make it Veggie! ◎

Just swap the chicken for other vegetables, like peas and broccoli, or use more potatoes instead of the chicken and follow the recipe in the same way.

 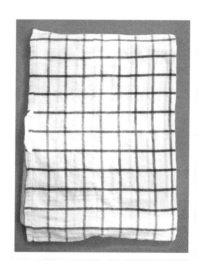 

  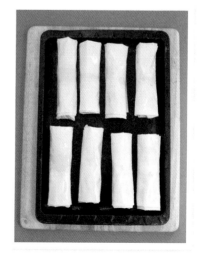

SWEETCORN AND CHORIZO CORNBREAD MUFFINS

PREP TIME: 15 minutes **BAKE TIME:** 15 minutes

Tasty little savoury muffins, brilliant in packed lunches or served with soup, chilli or a salad. They are delicious warm from the oven.

MAKES 12

- 100g **chorizo**, finely chopped
- 75g **plain flour**
- 75g **polenta** or **cornmeal** (available in most supermarkets)
- 1 tablespoon **caster sugar**
- 1½ teaspoons **baking powder**
- ½ teaspoon **salt**
- 1 large free-range **egg**
- 300ml **soured cream**
- 200g **tinned sweetcorn**, drained
- 50g **Cheddar cheese**, grated

YOU WILL NEED

- ☐ Weighing scales
- ☐ 12-hole muffin tin
- ☐ Paper muffin cases
- ☐ Small frying pan
- ☐ Small bowl
- ☐ 2 large mixing bowls
- ☐ Wooden spoon
- ☐ Fork
- ☐ Muffin tin
- ☐ Dessertspoon
- ☐ Cooling rack

HOW TO DO IT

1. Fill the muffin tin with paper cases. Preheat the oven to 220°C/200°C fan/gas mark 7.

2. Ask an adult to help you fry the chorizo in a small frying pan for about 2 minutes – you won't need to add oil to the pan because there is plenty in the chorizo. Tip the cooked chorizo into a little bowl and leave to cool.

3. Combine the flour, polenta, sugar, baking powder and salt in a bowl and make a well in the centre using a wooden spoon. In another mixing bowl, combine the egg, soured cream, sweetcorn, cheese and chorizo. Pour the wet ingredients into the well of flour and mix using a fork until it has just come together. Be careful not to overmix it.

4. Spoon about 2 heaped dessertspoons of the mixture into each hole of the muffin tin. Make sure the muffin holes are evenly filled and you use up all of the mixture.

5. Ask an adult to put the tray in the oven and bake for 10–15 minutes. When they are cooked, they will be lovely and golden and a skewer will come out clean. Leave in the tin for 5 minutes, then turn onto a wire rack to cool. Serve them warm, or allow them to cool completely – either way, enjoy!

STORAGE: Store in an airtight container and eat within 2–3 days.

FABULOUS HERB SODA BREAD AND HOMEMADE BUTTER

PREP TIME: 15 minutes **BAKE TIME:** 25 minutes

Everybody loves good old bread and butter and this is the easiest and quickest bread in the world. My friend Tom Herbert, who is an awesome baker, makes the best soda bread. It goes perfectly with a mug of soup on Hallowe'en or Bonfire Night – warming and cosy for when it's dark and cold outside. What could be better?

MAKES 1 LOAF AND BUTTER TO SERVE 6

300g **plain flour**, plus extra for dusting

2 teaspoons **baking powder**

1 teaspoon **caster sugar**

1 teaspoon **salt**

1 teaspoon chopped **fresh rosemary** (optional)

250ml **buttermilk** (use shop-bought or follow the instructions for making your own)

2 small handfuls of **golden linseed**, 1 for the bread and 1 to decorate (optional)

FOR THE BUTTER
900ml **double cream**

YOU WILL NEED
☐ Large mixing bowl
☐ Weighing scales
☐ Large knife
☐ Baking tray

FOR THE BUTTER
☐ Large mixing bowl
☐ Whisk (preferably electric)
☐ Kitchen paper
☐ Greaseproof paper
☐ Measuring jug

SODA BREAD

1. Preheat the oven to 220°C/200° fan/gas mark 7. Lightly grease a baking tray.

2. Combine the flour and baking powder in a large mixing bowl, then stir in the sugar and salt (plus rosemary and 1 handful of golden linseed, if using).

3. Pour three-quarters of the buttermilk into the dry ingredients and stir the mixture with one hand. Bring the dough together but don't mix too much or it will be heavy. When you have finished, the dough should be soft and sticky. Add a bit of extra buttermilk if it feels too dry.

4. Lightly dust your worktop with flour and tip the dough out. Gently shape into a round loaf about the size of a side plate, without kneading it too much. Flip it over to coat with the flour.

5. With the help of an adult, use a knife to make a deep cross over the top of the loaf, then sprinkle with the linseed, if using. Put the loaf on your baking tray and ask an adult to put it in the oven. Bake for 25 minutes, then leave to cool for at least 10 minutes before eating. Enjoy a big chunk of warm soda bread with your own butter.

STORAGE: This type of bread is best eaten fresh on the day it's made.

IF YOU'RE MAKING BUTTER AND BUTTERMILK . . .

1. Put the double cream in a large bowl and beat, beat, beat! After about 7 minutes you will notice a change in the look and sound of the cream and it will begin to separate into butter and buttermilk. Keep beating until the butter is firm and the liquid has all come out.

2. Now squeeze the butter in your hands to get the excess out. If you are not using your butter straight away, rinse it well with cold water, pat dry with kitchen paper, wrap in greaseproof paper and store in the fridge.

3. Pour the buttermilk you now have into a measuring jug. If you don't have enough to make the soda bread, you can make up the quantity with milk, shop-bought buttermilk or yogurt.

VERY SPECIAL JACKET POTATOES

SERVES 4 HUNGRY PEOPLE

4 large **baking potatoes**

2 medium free-range **eggs**, beaten

50g **salted butter**

200g **Cheddar cheese**, grated

A pinch of **pepper**

Any extra ingredients you fancy – I like cooked bacon, broccoli, sweetcorn, pesto, smoked salmon … Experiment to find your favourite combination!

PREP TIME: 10 minutes   **BAKE TIME:** 1 hour 20 minutes

This may look like an ordinary jacket potato recipe, but it's not! The secret here is in the double-baking. Try them - they really are a very special jacket!

YOU WILL NEED

- ☐ Weighing scales
- ☐ Tin foil
- ☐ Baking tray
- ☐ Small sharp knife
- ☐ Dessertspoon
- ☐ Large mixing bowl
- ☐ Fork

HOW TO DO IT

1. Preheat the oven to 200°C/180°C fan/ gas mark 7.

2. Wrap each potato separately in foil, put them on a baking tray and ask an adult to help you put them in the oven. Bake for about 1 hour, until they are soft when pierced with a fork. Ask an adult to remove from the oven, unwrap and leave to sit for a few minutes until cool enough to handle.

3. Cut off a lid from each potato and set to one side. Use a dessertspoon to scoop out the inside of each potato into a mixing bowl – be careful not to tear the skins. Add the eggs, butter, cheese and pepper (and any extra ingredients you like) and mash together with a fork.

4. Spoon the mash back into the potato skins and place carefully back onto your baking tray. Put the lids on the tray too (but not on the potatoes as you want the tops to puff up and brown a little). Ask an adult to put them back in the oven for another 15-20 minutes.

5. When they are ready, put the potato lids back on top of their potatoes and serve immediately.

SPOOKY SPIDER AND MOVIE-TIME CUPCAKES

PREP TIME: 20 minutes   **BAKE TIME:** 25 minutes

This is one yummy sticky toffee cupcake with two brilliant ways of decorating.

YOU WILL NEED

- [ ] 12-hole muffin tin
- [ ] Weighing scales
- [ ] 12 cupcake cases (my favourite for the spooky cakes are the metallic ones in black, and I like red for the movie cakes)
- [ ] Small bowl
- [ ] Large mixing bowl
- [ ] Wooden spoon or electric hand-held mixer
- [ ] Large spoon
- [ ] Spoon, piping bag or ice cream scoop

MAKES 12 CAKES

100g **dates**, chopped

80ml **hot water** (from a freshly boiled kettle)

1 teaspoon **bicarbonate of soda**

85g softened **unsalted butter**

140g **muscovado sugar**

2 medium free-range **eggs**

180g **self-raising flour**

FOR THE ICING:

100g softened **unsalted butter**

175g **icing sugar**, sifted

75g shop-bought or homemade **toffee sauce**

FOR SPIDER DECORATION:

200g **black fondant icing**

8-10 long thin black **liquorice laces** or use more black fondant, rolled into long thin strips

Small tube of **white, red or yellow writing icing**

FOR MOVIE-TIME DECORATION:

250g **toffee popcorn**

1. Fill the 12-hole muffin tin with the paper cases. Preheat the oven to 180°C/160°C fan/gas mark 4.

2. Mix together the dates, hot water and bicarbonate of soda in a small bowl, then set aside to soak.

3. In another bowl, beat the butter and sugar together with a wooden spoon or an electric hand-held mixer until soft, creamy and pale. Add the eggs one at a time, mixing well between adding each one. Add the date mixture and stir until well combined. Gently fold in the flour with a large spoon.

4. Spoon the mixture into the cupcake cases, making sure they are evenly filled. Ask an adult to help you put the tin in the oven and bake for 20–25 minutes until they are springy to the touch. Transfer to a wire rack to cool, while you prepare your icing and decorations.

5. For the icing, beat the butter in a large bowl until very soft, then add the icing sugar and beat again until light and fluffy. Stir in the toffee sauce and put in the fridge to chill for about 10 minutes before you spread onto the cakes.

6. FOR SPOOKY SPIDER DECORATIONS: Roll out 12 large balls of black fondant the size of a Brussels sprout (for the spider's body) and 12 small ones (for the spider's head). Cut the liquorice into pieces about the same length as the bodies – you will need 96 pieces, 8 legs each for 12 spiders! Use a piping bag or a palette knife to pipe or spread the icing on top of each cake, then put your spiders together. Pipe on little beady white, red or yellow eyes.

FOR MOVIE-TIME POPCORN DECORATIONS: Use a piping bag or a palette knife to pipe or spread the icing on top of each cake, then load the top with popcorn. You can dip some of the popcorn in the icing to get the pyramid shape to stick.

STORAGE: Un-iced, the cakes can be kept in an airtight container for up to 4 days, but once iced they should be eaten within 1–2 days.

TROPICAL SUNSHINE LUNCHBOX BARS

MAKES 12 BARS

150g **unsalted butter**, plus extra for greasing

75g soft **light brown sugar**

200g **condensed milk**

250g **porridge oats**

75g **desiccated coconut**

100g **dried apricots**, finely chopped or snipped

75g **dried mango**, chopped or snipped

PREP TIME: 20 minutes   **BAKE TIME:** 20 minutes

When the holidays are over and it's back-to-school time, it's normal to feel a bit glum. So why not take a little ray of sunshine with you in your lunchbox?

YOU WILL NEED

- ☐ Weighing scales
- ☐ 23cm baking tin (or a small roasting tin is perfect)
- ☐ Tin foil
- ☐ Small saucepan
- ☐ Wooden spoon
- ☐ Non-stick baking parchment
- ☐ Spoon or spatula

HOW TO DO IT

1. Line your baking tin with foil, then grease the foil with some butter. Preheat the oven to 180°C/160°C fan/gas mark 3.

2. With the help of an adult, heat the butter, sugar and condensed milk in a small saucepan until the sugar has dissolved and the mixture is runny. Remove from the heat and set aside.

3. Put the oats, coconut, apricot and mango into a large mixing bowl and stir to combine. Pour the sugar and butter mixture over the dry ingredients and stir together with a wooden spoon.

4. Pour the mixture into your prepared tin and use the back of a spoon or a spatula to spread it out and make sure it is smooth and even. Ask an adult to put your tin in the oven and bake for 15–20 minutes, until golden.

5. When it is time to take it out of the oven, leave to cool in its tin for about 10 minutes, then cut it into bars. Allow to cool completely before eating.

STORAGE: These brilliant bars can be kept for up to 7 days in an airtight container.

TOFFEE APPLE TRAYBAKE WITH TOFFEE FROSTING

PREP TIME: 15 minutes   **BAKE TIME:** 40 minutes

This is the best treat to enjoy around a bonfire as you watch the fireworks. You'll have to take your gloves off though, because this cake is so sticky and delicious you'll want to lick your fingers!

MAKES 12 SLICES OF CAKE

Unsalted butter, for greasing
2 large **cooking apples**
Juice of 1 **lemon**
100g **dried apple**
175ml **sunflower oil**
3 medium free-range **eggs**, beaten
150g soft **light brown sugar**
50g **caster sugar**
200g **plain flour**
1½ teaspoons **baking powder**
1½ teaspoons **bicarbonate of soda**
1 teaspoon **ground cinnamon**
1 teaspoon **vanilla extract**
Pinch of **salt**

FOR THE ICING:

175g softened **unsalted butter**
325g **icing sugar**, sifted
100g shop-bought or homemade **toffee sauce** (see page 213)

YOU WILL NEED

☐ 23cm x 30cm traybake cake tin
☐ Weighing scales
☐ Non-stick baking parchment
☐ Apple corer or sharp knife
☐ Cling film
☐ Measuring jug
☐ Whisk
☐ Scissors
☐ Wooden spoon
☐ Sieve
☐ Large mixing bowl
☐ Small mixing bowl
☐ Palette knife or spatula

1. Butter and line the cake tin with non-stick baking parchment. Preheat the oven to 180°C/160°C fan/gas mark 4.

2. Ask an adult to help you core and roughly chop the apples, then grate them into a mixing bowl. Squeeze the lemon juice over the apple, cover the bowl with cling film and set aside.

3. Measure the oil in a measuring jug, then pour this into another mixing bowl. Add both of the sugars and the vanilla and mix with a whisk until is light and airy. Add the beaten eggs to the sugar mixture a little at a time, whisking in between each addition.

4. Now you need your apple bowl back. With your hands, squeeze most of the juice from the apples, then snip up your dried apple using a pair of scissors. Add both of these to the sugar and egg mixture, stirring gently with a wooden spoon.

5. Sift the flour, baking powder, bicarbonate of soda and cinnamon into the bowl and fold through, making sure it's all incorporated. Pour your mixture into the prepared tin and smooth the top so it looks nice and even.

6. Ask an adult to put the cake in the oven and bake for 35–40 minutes until it is risen and springy to touch and a skewer comes out clean. Leave your cake in the tin for 10 minutes, then turn out onto a wire rack to cool.

7. For the icing, beat the butter until very soft in a large bowl, then add the icing sugar and beat again until light and fluffy. Stir in the toffee sauce and put in the fridge to chill for about 10 minutes, or until your cake has cooled. Then use a spatula or knife to spread the toffee icing over the top.

STORAGE: Store the cake in an airtight container and eat within 5 days.

P.S. Check out the toffee sauce recipe on page 213.

SIMPLY SPLENDID BAKED APPLES

PREP TIME: 10 minutes **BAKE TIME:** 40 minutes

A fuss-free, delicious recipe – and a brilliant, easy pud for a cold day. Mmmm.

MAKES 6

6 small **cooking apples**

50g **unsalted butter,** softened

100g **soft brown sugar**

1 teaspoon **ground cinnamon**

100g **dried cranberries**

75g **raisins**

Grated zest of 1 **orange**

2 tablespoons **Demerara sugar**

2 tablespoons **rolled oats**

YOU WILL NEED

☐ Ovenproof dish or small roasting tin

☐ Weighing scales

☐ Kitchen paper

☐ Apple corer

☐ Small sharp knife

☐ Small mixing bowl

☐ Wooden spoon

☐ Tin foil

1. Lightly butter your dish or roasting tin. Wash your apples, then dry them with some kitchen paper. Preheat the oven to 200°C/180°C fan/gas mark 6.

2. Ask an adult to help you take the core out of your apples (use a corer if you have one or a sharp knife if not). Then ask them to score the skin around the middle of the apples in a ring – this will stop the apple skins from bursting as they bake. Place the apples in your prepared dish or tin.

3. Beat the butter, sugar, cinnamon and orange zest together in a bowl with a wooden spoon. Add the dried fruit and mix this in too.

4. Push your buttery, sugary fruit mixture into the cored-out holes in the apples – you need to really stuff it in and pack it nice and tightly. If there is any mixture left over, just pile it on top of each apple. Sprinkle the oats and Demerara sugar over the top.

5. Cover the tin with foil and ask an adult to help you put your apples in the oven and bake for 20 minutes. Then remove the foil and bake for a further 15-20 minutes until the apples are lovely and soft. Serve immediately.

☆ Top Tip! ☆

These are delicious straight from the oven as they are or with a blob of natural yogurt. But my family like them with ice cream AND custard! Why not try them both ways and see which you prefer?

PEAR AND PECAN CRUMBLE

PREP TIME: 20 minutes **BAKE TIME:** 30–40 minutes

Another perfect pudding for a chilly autumn day. Crumble is usually made with apples, but for this special recipe, I think pears deserve a moment in the crumble spotlight.

SERVES 6

75g **unsalted butter**, chilled and cut into small cubes, plus extra for greasing

75g **pecans**

8–9 **ripe pears**

1 **lemon** (you will need the zest of the whole lemon and the juice of half of it)

3 tablespoons **maple syrup** plus extra for drizzling

150g **plain flour**

½ teaspoon **baking powder**

75g **golden caster sugar**

YOU WILL NEED

☐ Baking tray
☐ Weighing scales
☐ Small bowl
☐ Peeler
☐ Sharp knife
☐ Ovenproof dish
☐ Zester or fine grater
☐ Cling film

1. Lightly butter an ovenproof dish. Preheat the oven to 190°C/170°C fan/gas mark 5.

2. Put the pecans on a baking tray and ask an adult to toast them in the oven for about 5–10 minutes. Check them after 5 minutes to make sure they don't burn – you will be able to smell them when they are lovely and toasty. Ask an adult to take them out of the oven, then pour into a little bowl to cool. When they are cool enough to handle, chop them roughly. Turn the oven down to 170°C/150°C/gas mark 3.

3. Ask an adult to help you peel the pears and cut them into pieces, then put them into your ovenproof dish.

4. Grate the zest of the lemon over the pears, then cut the lemon in half and squeeze the juice of one half over the pears too. Spoon the maple syrup over and toss everything together with clean hands or a spoon. Cover with cling film and set aside.

5. To make the crumble, put the flour and baking powder into a bowl, then add the butter and rub into the flour with your fingertips until the mixture looks like breadcrumbs. Finally, stir in the sugar and chopped nuts.

6. Sprinkle the crumble over the pears, drizzle with a little more maple syrup, and ask an adult to put the dish in the oven for 30–40 minutes until the top is golden brown. Serve hot with fresh cream or ice cream.

STORAGE: Store any leftovers in the fridge for up to 7 days.

@ Try Something Different! @

Swap the pear for plum and the pecans for almonds. Or if you can't resist the good old apple, try it with hazelnuts.

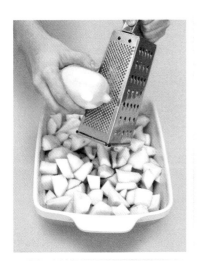

CINNAMON SWIRL PLUM TARTS

PREP TIME: 30 minutes **BAKE TIME:** 20 minutes

This recipe has swirly cinnamon puff pastry with juicy sweet plums. A posh autumn bake – yummy-plummy-in-my-tummy!

MAKES 12 TARTS

6 large, slightly **under-ripe red plums**

6 tablespoons **golden caster sugar**

Icing sugar, for dusting

1 x 375g pack ready-rolled **puff pastry**

50g very soft **unsalted butter**

2 tablespoons **ground cinnamon**

½ teaspoon **ground ginger**

1 free-range **egg**, beaten

YOU WILL NEED

☐ Weighing scales
☐ 2 baking trays
☐ Non-stick baking parchment
☐ Small sharp knife
☐ Sieve
☐ Knife, palette knife or spoon
☐ Rolling pin
☐ Spatula
☐ Pastry brush
☐ Palette knife or fish slice

1. Line 2 baking trays with non-stick baking parchment. Preheat the oven to 200°C/180°C fan/gas mark 4.

2. Ask an adult to cut the plums in half around the stone, then pull out the stones. Put the plums in a large mixing bowl and sprinkle over 3 tablespoons of the caster sugar. Use your hands to mix and rub the plums in the sugar. Tip the plums into a sieve, rest this on top of the bowl that you sugared the plums in and set aside while you make the swirly pastry.

3. Dust the worktop with a little icing sugar, then unroll the sheet of pastry and position with one of the short sides facing you.

4. Beat the butter, sugar, cinnamon and ginger together in a small bowl, then spread this mixture all over the pastry sheet using a knife or the back of spoon. Now from the short side closest to you, roll up the pastry like a Swiss roll, then slice and divide into 12 equal slices.

5. Dust the worktop with a little more icing sugar. Flatten each disc of pastry a little with the palm of your hand and roll them out until they are about the size of a saucer.

7. Place the plums cut-side down on your prepared baking trays – 6 on each is best – and place a swirly pastry disc over each plum. Use your hands to wrap the pastry around the plums, being careful not to stretch it too much or make holes in it. You will be left with a swirly pastry mound with a slightly ruffled rim of pasty around the bottom of the plums.

8. Brush your pastries with a little beaten egg and ask an adult to help you put them in the oven. Bake for 20 minutes, until the pastry is golden, puffy and cooked through and the plums are soft and juicy. Leave to rest for 2 minutes, because the plums will be very hot.

9. Use a palette knife or fish slice to release the tarts. Dust with a little icing sugar and serve.

STORAGE: Best served warm from the oven, but will keep for up to 2 days in the fridge.

@ Try Something Different! @

Swap the plums for nectarines. Just add the seeds from a vanilla pod to the pastry instead of the cinnamon and bake for an extra 5-10 minutes.

☆ Top Tip! ☆

You can eat these hot or cold – but I like them best warm from the oven!

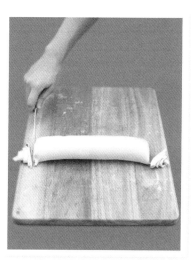

HAZELNUT TOFFEE CRISPY BARS

PREP TIME: 10 minutes   **CHILL TIME:** 30 minutes

An easy to remember recipe and no baking (I know - ssshh). These nutty, sticky, delicious bars are perfect for when you want something sweet in super-quick time. Wrap them up and take on autumn walks for an energy-boosting treat.

MAKES 24 BARS

100g **unsalted butter**
100g **toffees**
100g **white mini marshmallows**
100g **rice crispies**
100g **roasted chopped hazelnuts** (you can buy these from any good supermarket)

YOU WILL NEED

- [ ] Baking tray or small tin
- [ ] Weighing scales
- [ ] Non-stick baking parchment
- [ ] Large saucepan (preferably heavy-based)
- [ ] Wooden spoon
- [ ] Knife or spatula
- [ ] Sharp knife

1. Butter a baking tray or small tin and line with non-stick baking parchment.

2. Ask an adult to help you heat the butter, toffees and marshmallows in your saucepan over low heat, until melted and mixed (be very careful of boiling sugar). Remove the pan from the heat and stir in the rice crispies and hazelnuts.

3. Spread the mixture onto your prepared baking tray or tin and use a knife or spatula to shape into a rectangle – don't worry too much about neatness here. Leave to set for 30 minutes. Ask an adult to help you cut into bars and enjoy.

STORAGE: Store these in an airtight container and eat within 5 days.

BANUDGE BREAD

PREP TIME: 20 minutes **BAKE TIME:** 40-45 minutes

We love this banana-fudgy bread in our house. It's especially brilliant if your bananas get too ripe to eat - instead of throwing them in the bin, you can use them up in this totally tasty way.

MAKES 1 LOAF

150g **unsalted butter**, softened, plus extra for greasing

175g soft **light brown sugar**

2 medium free-range **eggs**, lightly beaten

3 very **ripe bananas**, mashed

2 tablespoons **buttermilk**

250g **plain flour**

2 teaspoons **baking powder**

1 teaspoon **vanilla extract**

100g **vanilla fudge**, cut into small chunks

YOU WILL NEED

- ☐ 900g loaf tin
- ☐ Weighing scales
- ☐ Non-stick baking parchment
- ☐ Large mixing bowl
- ☐ Fork
- ☐ Wooden spoon or electric hand-held mixer
- ☐ Large metal spoon
- ☐ Palette knife

HOW TO DO IT

1. Grease and line your loaf tin with non-stick baking parchment. Preheat the oven to 180°C/160°C fan/gas mark 4.

2. Cream the butter and the sugar together in a large mixing bowl until soft, pale and creamy. You can do this with a wooden spoon or an electric hand-held mixer if you have one. Add the lightly beaten eggs a little bit at a time, beating in between each addition.

3. Mix the banana, buttermilk and vanilla into the mixture one ingredient at a time, stirring gently, until it is all combined.

4. Add the flour and baking powder and use a large metal spoon to fold it into the mixture. Finally, fold through the fudge pieces.

5. Pour the mixture into the prepared loaf tin and smooth the top with the back of a spoon or a palette knife so it's nice and even.

6. Ask an adult to help you put the loaf in the oven and bake for 40–45 minutes until the loaf is springy to the touch and a skewer comes out clean.

7. Leave the loaf to cool in its tin for 10–15 minutes before turning out onto a wire rack to cool completely.

STORAGE: This cake stays lovely and moist and will keep in an airtight container for 3–5 days.

☆ Top Tip! ☆
If you can't find buttermilk, just mix 1 tablespoon of milk with 1 tablespoon of natural yogurt for the same flavour.

DROP SCONES
WITH BRAMBLE BUTTER AND FRESH BLACKBERRIES

PREP TIME: 10 minutes **BAKE TIME:** 10 minutes

My favourite time to make drop scones is on a Sunday afternoon in late September. Why not go out for a walk together and collect your own blackberries? You'll deserve these yummy treats after all that hard work!

MAKES ABOUT 30 SCONES

30g **unsalted butter**

200g **self-raising flour**

Pinch **salt**

25g **caster sugar**

2 free-range **eggs**, lightly beaten

300ml **whole milk**

A few drops of **sunflower oil** for frying

FOR THE BRAMBLE BUTTER

75g **unsalted butter**

3 tablespoons **blackberry jam**

1 tablespoon **honey**

A punnet of **fresh blackberries**

YOU WILL NEED

- [ ] Big frying pan or griddle pan
- [ ] Weighing scales
- [ ] Sieve
- [ ] Large mixing bowl
- [ ] Measuring jug
- [ ] Whisk
- [ ] Wooden spoon or electric hand-held mixer
- [ ] Cling film
- [ ] Pastry brush or kitchen paper
- [ ] Serving spoon
- [ ] Palette knife or fish slice
- [ ] Warm plate
- [ ] Clean tea towel

1. With the help of an adult, melt the butter in a saucepan over a low heat, then remove from the heat and set aside.

2. Sift the flour and salt into a large mixing bowl, then add the sugar and stir. Add the eggs and about two-thirds of the milk, then gently whisk the mixture together. When it looks like a smooth paste, pour in the melted butter and whisk again.

3. Now add the rest of the milk – do this a little at a time, until you have a mixture that is quite thick, but still nice and smooth. Set aside.

4. To make the bramble butter, use a wooden spoon to soften the butter. Then add the honey and jam and gently mix to combine. Cover with cling film and put it in the fridge.

5. Now it's time to make your scones. Ask an adult to put your frying pan on the hob and use a pastry brush or some kitchen paper to smear it with a drop of sunflower oil. Turn the hob to a medium heat and let the pan get hot.

6. Use a large serving spoon to spoon blobs of mixture into the pan – they will spread out into circles. You should be able to do 3 or 4 in the pan at the same time.

7. After about a minute, little bubbles will appear on the surface. When lots of bubbles have appeared, it's time to turn your scones over, using a palette knife or a fish slice. The second side always cooks quicker, so will only need about 30 seconds.

8. Use your palette knife to remove the scones from the pan, put them on a warm plate and cover with a clean tea towel to keep warm. Repeat until you have used up all the batter.

9. When you're ready to eat, spread your drop scones with bramble butter, then scatter over some fresh blackberries and a little extra sugar. What a treat!

STORAGE: These are most delicious fresh and warm from the pan, but they can be stored in a container for up to 3 days. Any leftover butter can be stored covered in the fridge for 2-3 days.

Cathryn Says:

Don't worry if your drop scones stick to the pan at first. My mum says, 'The first one or two drop scones always stick, because the pan is getting warmed up to make perfect ones.' You can just eat these ones to test them!

WINTER

CHEEKY LITTLE CHICKEN POT PIES

PREP TIME: 20 minutes **BAKE TIME:** 25 - 30 minutes

Filled with chicken, and with a crunchy pastry top, these are ideal for using up leftover chicken from your Sunday roast. So give grown-ups Monday night off, and have a go yourself!

MAKES AROUND 4–5 SMALL POT PIES

5 tablespoons **plain flour**, plus extra for dusting

1 x 375g pack (1 sheet) of ready-rolled **puff pastry**

3 tablespoons **unsalted butter**

1 small **onion**, finely chopped

1 **celery** stick, finely chopped, string peeled off

2 large **carrots**, finely chopped

A pinch of **fresh thyme** leaves

300g **cooked chicken**

150g **frozen peas**

200g **tinned sweetcorn**, drained

500ml **chicken stock**

1 medium free-range **egg**, beaten

Salt and **pepper**

YOU WILL NEED

☐ Weighing scales
☐ 4-5 x individual pie dishes (or 1 medium-sized ovenproof dish)
☐ Small sharp knife
☐ Table knife
☐ Large saucepan
☐ Wooden spoon
☐ Whisk
☐ Measuring jug
☐ Spoon
☐ Baking tray

HOW TO DO IT

1. Preheat the oven to 190°C/170°C/ gas mark 5.

2. Lightly dust your worktop with flour and lay out your pastry tray. Place one of your pie dishes upside down on the pastry and cut around with a knife. Your lids need to be roughly the same shape and size as your dishes but just a little bigger. Repeat for the other pie dishes. Set aside. (If you're doing one big pie, you only need to do this once.)

3. With the help of an adult, gently melt the butter in a saucepan over a medium heat. Add the onion, celery, carrots and thyme and cook for about 5 minutes, until the vegetables start to soften.

4. Add the flour and cook for 2 minutes, stirring continuously. Now add the stock, a little at a time, but keep stirring so that it doesn't become lumpy. When you have added all the stock, season with salt and pepper. Add the chicken, peas and sweetcorn and stir everything together.

5. Divide the filling equally into your 4 or 5 pots (or one big one) – ask an adult for help if you need it – then set them aside.

6. Cut a small cross in the middle of each lid with a knife – this is to let the steam out and stop the pastry getting soggy. Put your pastry lids carefully on top of each filled dish and brush with beaten egg.

7. Put the dishes on a baking tray and ask an adult to put them in the oven. Bake for 25-30 minutes until the pastry is crisp and the filling is bubbling hot. Enjoy straight away with broccoli and mashed potatoes for a delicious supper.

☆ Top Tip! ☆

Brushing the top
of your pies with
beaten egg will give
them a lovely shiny
golden finish.

SMASHING SAUSAGE ROLLS

PREP TIME: 10 minutes **BAKE TIME:** 25–30 minutes

Who doesn't love a sausage roll? I can't eat sausage rolls without brown sauce, which is why I've included it here, but feel free to leave it out – or replace with chutney, mustard or even ketchup.

MAKES 16

Unsalted butter, for greasing

8 good-quality **sausages**

3 tablespoons **brown sauce** – or pickle, mustard or chutney! (optional)

Plain flour, for dusting

1 x 500g block of **puff pastry** (not ready-rolled)

1 medium free-range **egg**, beaten with 1 teaspoon **HP sauce**

YOU WILL NEED

☐ Baking tray
☐ Scissors
☐ Weighing scales
☐ Mixing bowl
☐ Wooden spoon
☐ Table knife
☐ Small sharp knife
☐ Rolling pin
☐ Pastry brush
☐ Fork
☐ Cooling rack

HOW TO DO IT

1. Lightly grease a baking tray. Preheat the oven to 200°C/180°C fan/gas mark 6.

2. Take your sausages, snip a hole in the skin and squeeze out the sausagemeat into a bowl. Add the brown sauce, mix with a wooden spoon, then set aside.

3. Lightly dust your worktop with flour and use a table knife to cut the pastry block in half. Dust this with a little flour, then roll one half of the pastry into a rectangle about the size of an A4 sheet of paper. Lay the pastry in front of you with a long side facing you.

4. Divide your sausage mix in half and use your hands to make one large sausage out of it. Lay the sausage along the bottom half of the pastry rectangle, leaving a little border right at the edge. Brush all around the edges of the pastry with a little of the beaten egg.

5. Fold the top half of the pastry towards you over the sausage, then use a fork to push down the border to seal it. Ask an adult to help trim with a sharp knife. You now have 1 giant sausage roll. Slice this into 8 smaller sausage rolls with the help of an adult.

6. Place the sausage rolls on your prepared baking tray. Then repeat the same steps with the other half of the pastry block and the rest of the filling.

7. Brush the sausage rolls with the remaining beaten egg and ask an adult to put them in the oven. Bake for 25–30 minutes, until the pastry is golden and the sausagemeat is cooked through. Ask an adult to take them out of the oven and transfer to a wire rack to cool. Enjoy with an extra blob of HP sauce if you like . . . I do!

STORAGE: If you can resist eating these straight away, let them cool completely and store in the fridge for up to 3 days.

> ☆ Top Tip! ☆
>
> The sausage rolls are really best eaten warm, so if you have kept some in the fridge, pop them in an oven preheated to 190°C/170°C fan/gas mark 5 when you're ready to eat them and reheat for about 15 minutes.

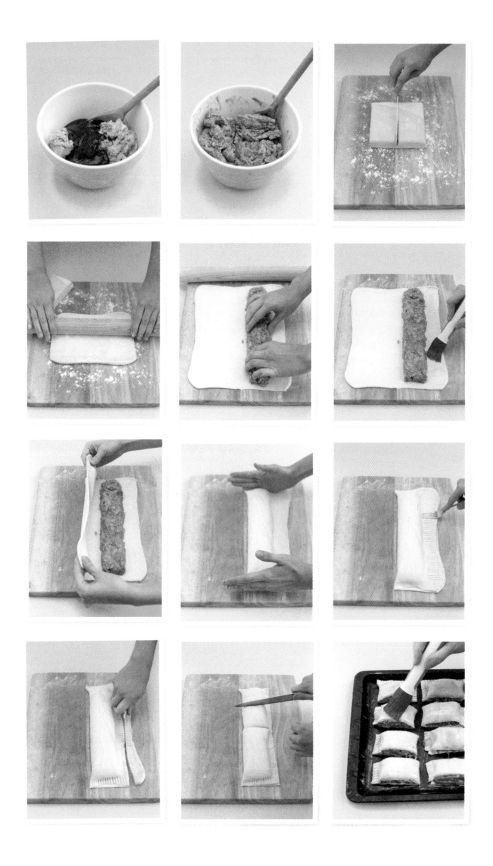

PETIT CROQUE-MONSIEUR CROISSANTS

PREP TIME: 10 minutes **BAKE TIME:** 15-20 minutes

These croissant-style pastries are stuffed with gooey cheese and tasty ham - great for a snack or as a yummy weekend breakfast.

MAKES 8

Unsalted butter, for greasing

Plain flour, for dusting

1 x 375g pack ready-rolled **puff pastry**

4 large British **ham** slices

200g **cheese**, grated (I like to use Gruyere)

1 medium free-range **egg**, beaten

YOU WILL NEED
- ☐ Grater
- ☐ Weighing scales
- ☐ Baking tray
- ☐ Table knife
- ☐ Pastry brush

1. Lightly grease a baking tray. Preheat the oven to 190°C/170°C fan/gas mark 5.

2. Dust the worktop with flour and lay out the pastry sheet with the longest side closest to you. Use a table knife to cut the pasty into quarters, so that you have 4 pastry rectangles. Now cut each of the rectangles from the top left-hand corner to the bottom right-hand corner. You should now have 8 pastry triangles.

3. Cut each slice of ham into 2 triangles in the same way as you have done the pastry and place 1 piece of ham on top of each pastry triangle. Sprinkle grated cheese over the ham on each triangle until you have used it all up.

4. Roll up the croissants, starting from the shortest edge of the triangle.

5. Carefully place the croissants on your prepared baking tray and brush with the beaten egg. Ask an adult to put them in the oven and bake for 15–20 minutes until the pastry has risen and looks golden and crispy.

STORAGE: Once baked these are best eaten straight away, but you can assemble and store unbaked ones in the fridge for 2-3 days (before baking).

@ Try Something Different! @

These croissants are delicious with all sorts of fillings. A few of my favourites are -

✳ Raspberry jam
✳ Dark and white chocolate chips
✳ Mozzarella and pesto
✳ Pecans and maple syrup
✳ Lemon curd

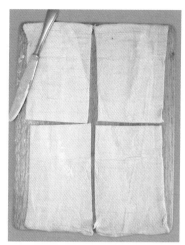

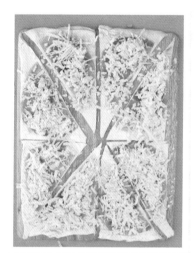

ENGLISH MUFFINS

PREP TIME: 30 minutes **BAKE TIME:** 15 minutes

English muffins are delicious at teatime, toasted and served with butter and cheese, or butter and jam. They are also brilliant filled with sausages and tomatoes at breakfast and make lovely sandwiches for lunch.

MAKES 10–12 MUFFINS

250ml **milk**

50ml **water**

25g **unsalted butter**

1 tablespoon **caster sugar**

1 teaspoon **salt**

425g **plain flour**, plus extra for dusting

1 x 7g sachet **fast-action yeast**

2 tablespoon **polenta** or **semolina**

YOU WILL NEED
- ☐ Heavy-based frying pan or griddle pan
- ☐ Weighing scales
- ☐ Small saucepan
- ☐ Large mixing bowl
- ☐ Wooden spoon
- ☐ Cling film
- ☐ Greaseproof paper
- ☐ Spatula or fish slice

1. Ask an adult to help you heat the milk, water and butter together in a small saucepan until it is lukewarm and the butter has melted. Remove from the heat and add the sugar and salt. Stir until it has dissolved.

2. In a large mixing bowl, combine the flour and yeast, then pour the milk mixture into the flour. Use a wooden spoon to combine, then roll up your sleeves and use your hands to bring it all together into a soft dough.

3. Lightly dust the worktop with flour, then tip your dough out and knead for about 10 minutes until you have a smooth, soft dough. Put the dough back into the bowl, cover with cling film and place somewhere warm for about 45–60 minutes, until it has doubled in size.

4. When your dough has risen, tip it back onto the lightly dusted worktop and leave to relax for a minute. Now divide into 10–12 pieces. Roll each piece into a neat ball and flatten into rounds about as thick as 2 fingers.

5. Sprinkle 1 tablespoon of the polenta or semolina over a large sheet of greaseproof paper, put the muffins on top, then sprinkle the other side with the rest of the polenta or semolina. Cover the muffins loosely in cling film until they have doubled in size again. This will take about 30 minutes.

6. Ask an adult to heat a large griddle or frying pan. When it is hot, you are ready to cook your muffins. Ask an adult to help you place 3 muffins at a time in the hot pan and cook for 2 minutes. Then, very gently, use a spatula to help you turn them over. The muffins will each take around 12–15 minutes to cook, and you will need to turn them every 2–3 minutes.

7. When the muffins are ready, they should be lightly browned on both sides and feel firm, but still springy. Remove from the pan and transfer to a wire rack to cool. Leave them for 2–3 minutes before you taste them.

STORAGE: Store in an airtight container and eat within 3 days. They are best cut in half and toasted after day 1.

BAKED SWEET 'N' SPICED PORRIDGE

SERVES 4

Unsalted butter, for greasing

150g **jumbo porridge oats**

800ml **milk**, plus extra to serve

60ml **condensed milk**

2 tablespoons **Demerara sugar**

A pinch of **grated nutmeg**

Small handful of **dried cranberries** (optional)

PREP TIME: 5 minutes **BAKE TIME:** 35 minutes

This is the most comforting wintery breakfast in the world. It is sweet and creamy, spiced and filling, cosy and EASY! It's also perfect as a pudding on a cold winter's evening, snuggled up on the sofa in dressing gowns and fluffy socks. Try it!

YOU WILL NEED

☐ Large ovenproof dish

☐ Spoon

☐ Weighing scales

☐ Measuring jug

☆ Top Tip! ☆

You can jazz your porridge up with dried fruit, nuts, honey, seeds, fresh fruit or even chocolate chips.

HOW TO DO IT

Hands OFF, Goldilocks

1. Grease a large ovenproof dish. Preheat the oven to 160°C/140°C fan/gas mark 3.

2. Add all the ingredients, except the sugar and nutmeg, to your dish and stir to combine. Leave to sit for 5 minutes until the oats start to soften and the flavours to begin to mix.

3. Sprinkle the sugar and nutmeg over the top and ask an adult to put the dish in the oven. Bake for 35 minutes until the top is golden and the oats are soft and creamy. Serve immediately.

MIDNIGHT BLACK CHOCOLATE LOAF CAKE

PREP TIME: 25 minutes   **BAKE TIME:** 45–50 minutes

This is a dark, sticky, chocolatey loaf cake. I call it 'Midnight' loaf because the little bits of white chocolate look like stars shining in the midnight sky – and because of the glittery gold stars it's decorated with!

MAKES 1 LOAF CAKE

Unsalted butter, for greasing

150g **plain flour**

50g **cocoa**

A pinch of **salt**

120ml **olive oil**

100g soft **light brown sugar**

60ml **black treacle**

60ml **golden syrup**

1 teaspoon **bicarbonate of soda**

80ml **hot water** (from a freshly boiled kettle – ask an adult to help)

3 medium free-range **eggs**, lightly beaten

100g **dark chocolate**, finely chopped

100g **white chocolate chips**

FOR THE GLAZE:

60ml **whole milk**

50g **unsalted tbutter**

1 tablespoon **golden syrup**

75g **dark chocolate**, broken into pieces

2 tablespoons **cocoa powder**

1 tablespoon **icing sugar**

Edible glittery gold stars, to decorate

YOU WILL NEED

☐ 900g loaf tin
☐ Weighing scales
☐ Non-stick baking parchment
☐ 2 small bowls or 1 small bowl and a mug
☐ Large mixing bowl
☐ Whisk
☐ Cooling rack
☐ Small saucepan
☐ Heatproof bowl
☐ Greaseproof paper

1. Grease the loaf tin with a little butter and cut strips of non-stick baking parchment to line the bottom and the sides of the tin. Preheat the oven to 170°C/150°C fan/ gas mark 3.

2. Put the flour, cocoa and salt into a small mixing bowl and set aside. Now, in a large mixing bowl, whisk together the oil, sugar, treacle and syrup until well combined – don't worry if it separates a little.

3. Put the bicarbonate of soda into a mug or small bowl and add the hot water – it will fizz and bubble, so stir gently, then pour into the oil and sugar mixture and whisk. Add the flour, cocoa and salt and continue to gently whisk until the ingredients are just combined. Add the eggs and whisk again. Finally, stir the dark and white chocolate through the mixture.

4. Pour this into the prepared loaf tin and ask an adult to put it in the oven to bake for 40–50 minutes, until a skewer comes out clean. Ask an adult to remove the cake from the oven and let your cake rest in the tin for 10 minutes, then turn it onto a wire rack to cool completely.

5. While your loaf cools, prepare the glaze. Ask an adult to help you heat the milk, butter and syrup in a small pan. Stir until everything is mixed together and the butter has melted.

6. Put the chocolate in a heatproof bowl, pour the hot milk and syrup mix over the chocolate and stir until melted. Then whisk in the cocoa powder and icing sugar and leave to cool and thicken a little.

7. When your cake has completely cooled, put some greaseproof paper under the cooling rack and pour the icing over the cake. This will catch any icing that runs over the side and save lots of mess. Sprinkle with the glittery gold stars to finish.

STORAGE: This cake will keep in an airtight container for 5–7 days

☆ Top Tip! ☆

If your icing is lumpy, pop your bowl over a pan of gently simmering water to melt the chocolate completely.

BANANA SANDWICH CUSTARD PUD'

PREP TIME: 30 minutes   **BAKE TIME:** 30 minutes

My 'bunch' and I love bananas – we especially love banana sandwiches and banana custard. And bread and butter pudding is one of our favourite puddings, so this is a combination of all of these things!

SERVES 6 (OR 4 HUNGRY MONKEYS)

75g soft **unsalted butter**, plus extra for greasing

10 slices of **white, medium-sliced bread**

2 large **ripe bananas**

50g **Demerara sugar**

2 large free-range **eggs**

50g **caster sugar**

1 teaspoon **vanilla extract** or vanilla bean paste

250ml **whole milk**

50ml **double cream** (or make up the milk to 300ml)

YOU WILL NEED

☐ 20cm ovenproof dish
☐ Weighing scales
☐ Knife
☐ Fork
☐ Whisk
☐ Small saucepan

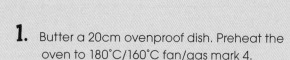

1. Butter a 20cm ovenproof dish. Preheat the oven to 180°C/160°C fan/gas mark 4.

2. Butter one side of each slice of bread. Don't worry about cutting the crusts off – some will go crunchy and delicious. Peel the bananas and ask an adult to help you thinly slice them.

3. Place about 12 slices of banana on the buttered side of one slice of bread, sprinkle with a little Demerara sugar, then top with another slice of bread. BUT this piece of bread needs to have the buttered side facing up! Repeat until you have used all the bread, banana and sugar.

4. Ask an adult to help you cut each of the sandwiches into 4 triangles, then arrange them overlapping one another in your buttered 20cm ovenproof dish.

5. Now make the custard. Beat the eggs, sugar and vanilla together in a bowl with a whisk until you have a frothy light mixture. With the help of an adult, heat the milk and cream (if using) in a small pan for a few minutes until it is almost boiling – you'll be able to tell because little bubbles will start to appear around the very edge of the pan. Pour the hot milk into the egg mixture slowly and whisk well.

6. Pour the custard over your sandwiches and give the sandwiches a little nudge to make sure they are properly covered in the custard. Set aside for about 20 minutes until the bread has soaked up the custard. Then sprinkle over a little more Demerara sugar and ask an adult to help you to put the dish in the oven. Bake for 30 minutes until the custard is set and the top of your pud' is golden with some crunchy corners. Serve immediately. This is lovely served with vanilla ice cream, or simply as it is.

CAT'S COOKIES

PREP TIME: 20 minutes **BAKE TIME:** 8–10 minutes

The best cookies should be a bit crunchy around the edge, but chewy in the middle – and these cookies are just that. They are quick and delicious, especially warm from the oven with a big glass of milk.

MAKES AROUND 12 BIG COOKIES

150g **unsalted butter**, very soft

75g **soft light brown sugar**

75g **caster sugar**

25g **dark soft brown sugar**

1 medium free-range **egg**

1 teaspoon **vanilla essence**

200g **plain flour**

½ teaspoon **baking powder**

A pinch of **salt**

100g **plain chocolate chips**

100g **milk chocolate chips**

YOU WILL NEED

- ☐ 2 baking trays
- ☐ Weighing scales
- ☐ Non-stick baking parchment
- ☐ Large mixing bowl
- ☐ Wooden spoon or an electric hand-held mixer
- ☐ Tablespoon
- ☐ Cooling rack
- ☐ Palette knife or fish slice

HOW TO DO IT

1. Line 2 baking trays with non-stick baking parchment. Preheat the oven to 190°C/170°C fan/gas mark 5.

2. Beat together the butter and the sugars in a large mixing bowl until just combined, using a wooden spoon, or an electric hand-held mixer if you have one.

3. Add the egg and vanilla and stir. Then add the flour and mix in thoroughly too. Finally add the chocolate chips and stir through. The mixture should be sticky and not too stiff. Put the cookie dough in the fridge for 10 minutes before baking.

4. Spoon heaped tablespoons of the mixture onto your prepared baking trays and flatten a little with your hand or the back of a spoon. Your cookies will flatten and spread while they are baking, so leave plenty of room between them.

5. Ask an adult to help you put the cookies into the oven and bake for 8–10 minutes. They will look pale in the middle and golden around the edges. This is what you want.

6. Give the cookies a minute or two on their trays to harden before transferring to a cooling rack (or they will fall apart), then use a palette knife to move them.

STORAGE: These cookies store for up to 7 days in an airtight container – although I will be impressed if you have enough willpower not to eat them on day 1!

☆ Top Tip! ☆

Don't be tempted to add any extra flour to your cookie dough or to bake them for longer than 10 minutes. If you do, they won't be soft and chewy.

◎ Try Something Different! ◎

How about adding oat and raisin, or white chocolate, or cranberry and orange?

LIDA'S LOVELY CZECH DAINTIES

PREP TIME: 10 minutes   **BAKE TIME:** 10–12 minutes

Lida is my sister-in-law and she is Czech. Her grandma and mother would make these vanilla biscuits at Christmas. We have named them 'Little Dainties' because they are sweet, nutty, sugary and dainty and they melt in your mouth. Děkuji, Lida! (Thanks, Lida!) x

MAKES LOTS OF LITTLE DAINTIES

250g **plain flour**

210g **unsalted butter**, very soft

100g **blanched chopped almonds** (buy them like this)

70g **icing sugar**

1 teaspoon **vanilla extract**

50g **icing sugar**, for dusting

YOU WILL NEED

☐ 2 baking trays

☐ Weighing scales

☐ Non-stick baking parchment

☐ Large mixing bowl

☐ Wooden spoon

☐ Teaspoon

☐ Shallow bowl (e.g. pasta bowl)

☐ Fork

HOW TO DO IT

1. Line 2 baking trays with non-stick baking parchment. Preheat the oven to 190°C/170°C fan/gas mark 5.

2. Mix all the ingredients in a large mixing bowl with a wooden spoon and then use your hands to form a ball of dough. Don't work the dough too much; you just need to bring it together. Chill the dough in the fridge for 10 minutes before shaping.

3. Take teaspoons full of the dough and roll into little balls, about the size of a Brussels sprout, then shape into little crescent moons. Place your dainties onto your prepared baking trays.

4. Ask an adult to help you put the trays in the oven and bake for 10–12 minutes. When they are ready they should be pale, but feel firm to touch.

5. Now put the icing sugar into a large shallow bowl (like a pasta bowl, for example). When the biscuits come out of the oven, leave them on the tray for about 5 minutes to cool, then toss or roll a few at a time in the bowl of icing sugar. The warmth of the biscuit will help the sugar to stick to them. When they are covered in sugar, lift them back onto the rack to cool completely.

STORAGE: Store in an airtight container, and eat within a week.

> ☆ Top Tip! ☆
>
> These little dainties are perfect to bake at Christmas and also make lovely gifts or after-dinner treats.

LEMONY RICE PUDDING

PREP TIME: 5 minutes **BAKE TIME:** 2 hours

I love, love, love rice pudding! This recipe is warming, simple and delicious - with a zingy lemon twist! It tastes even better with lemon curd and will keep you cosy on a cold day.

SERVES 6–8

Unsalted butter, for greasing
150g **pudding rice**
75g **caster sugar**
900ml **milk**
Grated **zest** of 1 large unwaxed **lemon**
Lemon curd, to serve

YOU WILL NEED

☐ 2 litre ovenproof dish
☐ Sieve
☐ Measuring jug
☐ Zester or fine grater

HOW TO DO IT

1. Lightly butter the ovenproof dish. Preheat the oven to 150°C/130°C fan/gas mark 2.

2. Put the rice in a large sieve and rinse under cold water. Tip the rice into the buttered dish, add the sugar, milk and lemon zest and stir all the ingredients together.

3. Ask an adult to help you put the dish in the oven and bake for 2 hours until it is has browned on top and is creamy underneath and the rice is soft. Serve in bowls with a big dollop of lemon curd.

STORAGE: Eat straight away.

GINGERBREAD SHAPES

PREP TIME: 5 minutes, plus chilling **BAKE TIME:** 10–12 minutes

This is the crispiest, tastiest gingerbread ever! It's perfect for making Christmas decorations. At my house, we make little shapes to hang on our tree with ribbon, but we have to hang them up high or our dog Lola tries to eat them – the rascal! But as they are so delicious, we can't really blame her!

MAKES ABOUT 15 GINGERBREAD SHAPES

2 tablespoons **golden syrup**

1 large free-range **egg yolk**

200g **plain flour**, plus extra for dusting

½ teaspoon **baking powder**

2 teaspoons **ground ginger**

1 teaspoon **ground cinnamon**

A pinch of **salt**

100g **unsalted butter**, cold and cut into cubes

50g **light soft brown sugar**

25g **caster sugar**

FOR THE ROYAL ICING:

500g **royal icing sugar**

75ml **water** (or follow the icing packet instructions)

Edible silver or white glitter

YOU WILL NEED

☐ 2 baking trays

☐ Weighing scales

☐ Non-stick baking parchment

☐ Small mixing bowl

☐ Whisk

☐ Large mixing bowl

☐ Wooden spoon

☐ Cling film

☐ Rolling pin

☐ Cookie cutters

☐ Cooling rack

☐ Disposable piping bag

☐ Scissors

1. Line 2 baking trays with non-stick baking parchment. Look out for the preheat the oven stage in Step 4.

2. Beat together the syrup and egg with a whisk in a small mixing bowl. Sift the flour, baking powder, ginger, cinnamon and salt into another mixing bowl, then add the butter and rub into the flour until it looks like breadcrumbs. Then add the sugar and stir. Finally, stir in the egg and syrup mixture until it starts to form a dough.

3. Gently gather the dough together with your hands, then tip it out onto a lightly floured worktop. Flatten it into a disc, wrap in cling film and put in the fridge for 1 hour. This will make it easier to roll and keep the shapes neat as they bake.

4. When the dough is chilled, preheat the oven to 170°C/150°C fan/gas mark 3.

5. Lightly dust the worktop with more flour, divide the dough in half and roll out the first half to about the thickness of a pound coin. Use your cookie cutter to cut out as many shapes as you can, keeping them as close together as possible. Repeat with the second half of the dough.

6. Place the shapes on the prepared baking trays and ask an adult to help you put them in the oven. Bake for 10–12 minutes until crisp and golden. When the gingerbread comes out of the oven, transfer to a wire cooling rack.

7. Let the gingerbread completely cool, then decorate. Make the royal icing as per the packet instructions, fill a disposable piping bag with the icing, snip off the tip and pipe onto your biscuit shapes. Sprinkle with edible glitter to finish.

STORAGE: Gingerbread that is hung on the tree will go a little stale after about a day, so the ones you want to eat are best stored in an airtight container and should be eaten within 5-7 days.

☆ Top Tip! ☆

For extra-colourful decorations, use food colour pastes or powders to brighten up your royal icing.

LITTLE TUBBY RASCALS

PREP TIME: 20 minutes   **BAKE TIME:** 15-20 minutes

My husband was born in the North East, and these tea-time treats are a twist on a famous recipe from this part of the country. They are a little like rock cakes and lovely on winter afternoons with a hot drink.

MAKES 12 LITTLE TUBBY RASCALS

100g **ground almonds**

200g **self-raising flour**

1 teaspoon **baking powder**

150g **unsalted butter**, cut into cubes

100g **light soft brown sugar**

1 teaspoon **ground cinnamon**

Zest of 1 **orange**

Zest of 1 **lemon**

150g **dried apricots,** chopped

100g **golden sultanas**

75ml **milk**

2 tablespoons **double cream**

1 medium free-range **egg**, beaten

TO DECORATE:

12 **cherries**

A handful of **raisins**

YOU WILL NEED

☐ Baking tray

☐ Non-stick baking parchment

☐ Weighing scales

☐ Sieve

☐ Small bowl

☐ Fork

☐ Large mixing bowl

☐ Zester or fine grater

☐ Pastry brush

☐ Spoon or ice cream scoop

1. Line the baking tray with non-stick baking parchment. Preheat the oven to 200°C/180°C/gas mark 6.

2. Sift the ground almonds, flour and baking powder into a bowl and rub in the butter using your fingers until the mixture looks like breadcrumbs. Stir in the sugar, cinnamon, zests and dried fruit.

3. Put the egg, milk and cream in a small bowl and whisk together with a fork. Pour this into the dry ingredients and stir gently with the fork until the dough comes together.

4. Spoon or scoop the dough into 12 balls onto your prepared baking tray.

5. Give each rascal a little face by pushing on raisin eyes and a big cherry nose. Ask an adult to help you put them in the oven and bake for 15–20 minutes until golden.

STORAGE: Store in an airtight container for 2-3 days, or these freeze well.

CHOCOLATE TRUFFLES

PREP TIME: 1 hour, plus chilling   **BAKE TIME:** none

It's just not Christmas without chocolate in the house - and these truffles make lovely gifts or after-dinner treats. Or you could leave them out for Father Christmas!

MAKES ABOUT 20 CHOCOLATES

200g **double cream**

50g **dark brown sugar**

Fresh peel of 1 large unwaxed **orange** (use a peeler to take strips of the peel, trying to get as little white pith as possible)

1–2 drops of **orange extract** (optional)

200g good-quality **dark chocolate**, finely chopped

FOR DUSTING AND ROLLING:

50g good-quality **cocoa powder**

50g **soft light brown sugar**, sieved

Some **edible gold, orange or bronze glitter**, to decorate

YOU WILL NEED
- ☐ Peeler
- ☐ Small saucepan
- ☐ Weighing scales
- ☐ Wooden spoon
- ☐ Sieve
- ☐ Large heatproof bowl
- ☐ Cling film
- ☐ Small bowl
- ☐ Baking parchment

P.S. No baking needed here, but these chocolates are so good, who cares?

HOW TO DO IT

1. Put the cream in a saucepan with the sugar, strips of orange peel and extract, if using, and stir. With the help of an adult, place the pan on a medium heat and bring the cream to the boil. Let it bubble for 1–2 minutes, then take it off the heat and leave to cool for a minute.

2. Put the chopped chocolate in a heatproof bowl and pour the cream through a sieve over the chocolate (the sieve will catch the orange peel). After about 30 seconds, start to whisk the mixture as the chocolate melts. You should end up with a smooth glossy chocolate ganache.

3. Cover the bowl with cling film and let the chocolate cool for 20 minutes at room temperature. Then put the bowl in the fridge and leave to set for about an hour.

4. When the ganache is firm, take it out of the fridge. Place the sugar and cocoa for dusting in a small mixing bowl and combine. You will need to keep this beside you for dipping your fingers in and for rolling the truffles in.

5. Use a teaspoon to scoop out balls of ganache and place them on a sheet of baking parchment in a cool dry place on your kitchen worktop. You are now ready to roll and dust your truffles.

6. Wash your hands in cold water and dry well, then dip your fingers in the cocoa-sugar mixture. Roll each of the truffles quickly into a ball with your fingers, then roll it in the cocoa and place back onto the sheet of greaseproof paper in a cool dry place.

7. Your truffles are now done, but you can decorate with a sprinkle of orange or bronze glitter to really make them look festive.

STORAGE: Store these in a cool dry place and eat within a few days.

☆ Top Tip! ☆

Keep the kitchen as cool as possible and work as quickly as you can so that the chocolate doesn't melt and you don't end up too messy.

☆ Top Tip! ☆

Have all of your ingredients prepared and ready before you start making the truffles.

OTHER YUMMY THINGS

MEGA SPEEDY, EASY PEASY ICE CREAM

SERVES 6–8

400ml **double cream**
150ml **condensed milk**
50ml **natural yogurt**
1 teaspoon **vanilla extract**
or vanilla bean paste

YOU WILL NEED

- ☐ 900g loaf tin
- ☐ Cling film
- ☐ Bowl
- ☐ Whisk or an electric hand-held mixer

PREP TIME: 10 minutes   **FREEZE TIME**: 2 hours

Try it with Baked Apples (p140), Pear and Pecan Crumble (p144) or Banana Sandwich Custard Pud' (p186).

 HOW TO DO IT

1. Line the loaf tin with cling film.

2. Put everything in a bowl and whisk, either by hand or with an electric mixer, until it becomes thick like softly whipped cream.

3. Pour the mixture into the lined loaf tin, cover with cling film and put it in the freezer for about 2 hours until it is frozen.

TOFFEE SAUCE

PREP TIME: 10 minutes

Mix in with the icing for Toffee Apple Traybake (p136) or enjoy with pancakes or over ice cream.

(p136)

MAKES 1 LARGE JAR
100g **unsalted butter**
200g **light soft brown sugar**
200g **golden syrup**
200ml **double cream**
½ teaspoon **vanilla extract**

YOU WILL NEED
☐ Small saucepan
☐ Wooden spoon

HOW TO DO IT

1. Ask an adult to put all the ingredients in a small saucepan, and stir over a medium heat until it boils.

2. Boil the mixture rapidly for around 4 minutes until thick. Pour into a bowl to cool.

STORAGE: Use your sauce within 5 days and store in the fridge. It will become much thicker when chilled so you can just stir it and leave it to come to room temperature before you want to use it.

FRUITY SMOOTHIES

PREP TIME: 5 minutes

Fruity treats, perfect for summer.

HOW TO DO IT

Put the ingredients for your chosen smoothie flavour in a blender and blitz. Pour into glasses and enjoy straight away.

SERVES 2

BERRYLICIOUS:
300g **frozen summer berries**
250ml **milk**
100ml **natural yogurt**
2 tablespoons **honey**

SUNBEAM SPLENDOUR:
250g prepared **fresh mango**
400ml **orange and passionfruit juice**
6–7 **ice cubes**

YOU WILL NEED
☐ Blender or food processor
☐ Glasses

CUPS OF COSINESS

PREP TIME: 5 minutes

Just the thing for when the nights start to get chilly.

FOR THE WARM VANILLA MILK:

400ml **milk**

1 teaspoon **vanilla extract**

1 tablespoon **sugar**

FOR THE HEAVENLY HOT CHOCOLATE:

350ml **milk**

50ml **double cream**

½ tablespoon **light muscavado sugar**

50g **good-quality dark chocolate** (about 70% cocoa solids), finely chopped

HOW TO DO IT

YOU WILL NEED
☐ Saucepan
☐ Whisk

WARM VANILLA MILK

With the help of an adult, heat everything in a saucepan and whisk until frothy.

HEAVENLY HOT CHOCOLATE

With the help of an adult, heat the milk, cream and sugar in a saucepan until almost boiling. Remove from the heat, add the chocolate, leave it for 30 seconds, then whisk to melt the chocolate and make it nice and frothy.

DELICIOUS DIPS

PREP TIME: 10-15 minutes

These are great with Pitta Pockets (p68) and as part of a picnic.

HOW TO DO IT

HUMMUS

YOU WILL NEED
☐ Food processor

1. Put all ingredients in a food processor and blitz until smooth. Sprinkle with a little extra paprika before serving.

YOGHURT, CUCUMBER AND MINT DIP

YOU WILL NEED
☐ Grater
☐ Mixing bowl

1. With help from an adult, cut the cucumber in half lengthways and scoop out the seeds. Then grate the cucumber into a bowl and sprinkle the salt over it. Leave for 10 minutes.

2. In another bowl, stir together all the other ingredients.

3. Squeeze the water out of the cucumber with your hands and stir into the yogurt mix. Sprinkle with paprika before serving.

STORAGE: Store both dips, covered, in the fridge and eat within 2-3 days.

SERVES 4

FOR THE HUMMUS:

1 x 400g tin of **chickpeas**, drained

1 small or ½ large **garlic clove**, finely chopped

½ teaspoon **salt**

½ teaspon **smoked paprika**, plus extra for sprinkling

3 tablespoons **olive oil**

1 heaped tablespoon smooth **peanut butter** (optional)

Juice of 1 **lemon**

FOR THE YOGHURT, CUCUMBER AND MINT DIP:

1 **cucumber**

½ teaspoon **salt**

350ml **Greek yogurt**

2 tablespoons freshly squeezed **lemon juice**

Handful of chopped **fresh mint**

A dash of **olive oil**

Smoked paprika, for sprinkling

QUICK STRAWBERRY JAM

PREP TIME: 15 minutes

A super-quick jam to go with lots of the recipes in this book - like Wonderful White Loaf (p34) or Super Scones (p38).

MAKES 1 JAR

300g hulled (minus the green bits!) **strawberries**
50g **caster sugar**
A little squeeze of **lemon juice**

YOU WILL NEED

☐ Food processor
☐ Small saucepan
☐ Weighing scales
☐ Spoon
☐ Sterilised jar

HOW TO DO IT

1. Put the strawberries in a food processor and blitz until smooth. Pour this into a pan and add the sugar and lemon. Ask an adult to bring this mixture to the boil, then continue to boil for 10 minutes.

2. Using a spoon, scoop off any white or grey bubbles that stay on the surface.

3. Pour the mixture into the jar, allow to cool then keep in the fridge and use within 2 weeks.

INDEX

A

adult help 13

B

baked apples 140–3

baked eggs with soldiers 24–5

baked porridge 180–1

banana sandwich custard pud 186–9

banudge bread 154–7

baps 42–5

biscuits

Cat's cookies 190–3

cheese and chive biscuits 16–19

Czech dainties 194–7

gingerbread shapes 200–3

hazelnut toffee crispy bars 152–3

honey bee biscuits 104–7

lunchbox bars 134–5

malty moon custard biscuits 94–7

shortbread 62–5

bread

baps 42–5

herb soda bread 124–7

iced buns 44

muffins 176–9

pittas 68–71

pizza 78–81

rolls 36

white loaf 34–7

butter

bramble butter 160

creaming with sugar 11

making butter 126

rubbing into flour 8

buttermilk 126

substitute 156

buzzy bee decorations 106

C

cakes

banudge bread 154–7

carrot cake 50–3

chocolate brownies 112–15

chocolate loaf cake 182–5

cupcakes 130–3

friendship chain cake 88–93, 223

jam tarts 98–9

meringues 108–11

Scan or photocopy these instructions to give to your friends along with their Friendship Chain Cake Starter batter.

FRIENDSHIP CAKE INSTRUCTIONS

I am your very own Friendship Chain Cake Starter. I am alive and need looking after. I need to sit on your worktop for 10 days without a lid on, and away from draughts so I don't get too cold. Please don't put me in the fridge or I will fall asleep, like a hibernating bear. If I stop bubbling, I am too sleepy to keep.

GROW YOUR BATTER

FOR FEEDING THE MIX
300g **plain flour**
400g **caster sugar**
480ml **milk**

Day 1: Put your cake batter into a large mixing bowl and cover loosely with a clean tea towel.

Day 2: Stir well

Day 3: Stir well

Day 4: Feed your cake mix. Add half the plain flour, half the caster sugar and half the milk. Stir well.

Day 5: Stir well

Day 6: Stir well

Day 7: Stir well

Day 8: Stir well

Day 9: Add the remaining ingredients and stir well. Divide the batter into 4 equal portions. Keep 1 portion for yourself and give the other 3 to 3 more friends, along with a copy of these instructions. Keep your mix covered with a clean tea towel until tomorrow when you can bake with it.

Day 10: Hooray – you are ready to make your cake!

BAKE YOUR FRIENDSHIP CHAIN CAKE

50g **unsalted butter**
2 **cooking apples**, peeled, cored and chopped into small cubes
200g **caster sugar**
300g **plain flour**
Pinch of **salt**
2 teaspoons **baking powder**
2 medium free-range **eggs**, beaten
2 teaspoons **vanilla extract**
1 teaspoon **ground cinnamon**
100g dried **blueberries**
100g fresh **blueberries**
50g **Demerara sugar**

1. Preheat the oven to 180°C/ 160°C fan/gasmark 6. Grease and line the cake tin with non-stick baking parchment.

2. Ask an adult to help you melt the butter in a small saucepan over a low heat, then add to your cake batter, along with all the other ingredients except for the Demerara sugar and the fresh blueberries. Mix until well combined. Then add the blueberries and stir.

3. Pour the mixture into your prepared cake tin and sprinkle the Demerara sugar over the top.

4. Ask an adult to put the cake in the oven and bake for 45–50 minutes until golden and springy to the touch. If you test the middle with a skewer, it should come out clean. If not, put it back in the oven for a couple more minutes.

5. Leave the cake in the tin for 5 minutes to cool, then turn out on to a wire rack to cool completely.

STORAGE: The baked cake will keep for up to 7 days in an airtight container.

ACKNOWLEDGMENTS

My chance to say some (lots of) humungous 'thank you's!

To everyone and everything 'Bake Off', you made my dreams come true;
and Love Productions, you have been kind and genius. I wish I could list you all,
but here are just some; Amanda, Sam, Tallulah, Faenia, Nina, Mel, Sue, Paul and the
magnificent Mary. And to my extra special star-baker friends, John, James and SJ!

To Tom Herbert and Paul A Young, who have given their time,
knowledge and inspiration so generously.

To Emanuele and Stuart, for help and guidance.

To the totally awesome peanuts that I know and love (some of whom have snuck into
this book), Scarlett, Ruby, Klara, Jenny, Ellie, Evie, Ben, Ashley, Claudia, Jaimeson, Thomas,
George, Bo, Oakly, Saffron, Oliver, Luke, Otto and Lola.

To KitchenAid and Pampered Chef, for such glorious bits of kit that
feature throughout Let's Bake.

To Mike, Vicky and Emily at Just Scrumptious, and the Cornerstone Café ladies.

To my precious family, Ange and Dale, Stuey and Gemma, Ali and Lida. Inspirational Aunties,
Auntie, Sally and Jill. And to Grandad, who I know would think this book is pretty cool!

To Andrea, for being the best friend.

Very Importantly . . .

To the awe-inspiring team who I was blessed to have working on this book.
You managed to dip into my messy thoughts and perfectly turned my visions and
ideas into an actual book full of wonderful photos, doodles and fun,
I love it . . . you clever badgers!!! Jenny, Lu, Abi and Kate, you are all incredible!

Lastly and at the top of my voice . . .

To Craigie, my bestest and my rock!

To Mum, without you I would be rubbish, you have always
given me everything, you're the best.

AND

To my MAISIE and AMBROSE, you are my EVERYTHING!!!

I love you all, you lovely lot!
THANKS A MILLION